I Knew That!

Remembering Life's Lessons from Proverbs

Mike Root

COVENANT PUBLISHING

Copyright © 2003 by Mike Root

Published by Covenant Publishing

www.covenantpublishing.com

Covenant Publishing
P.O. Box 390 Webb City, Missouri 64870
Call toll free at 877.673.1015

Printed and Bound in the
United States of America
All Rights Reserved

All Scripture quotations, unless otherwise indicated, are taken from the NEW AMERICAN STANDARD BIBLE®, Copyright © 1960, 1962, 1968, 1971, 1972, 1973, 1975, 1977, 1995 by The Lockman Foundation. Used by permission.

Library of Congress Cataloging-in-Publication Data

Root, Mike.
  I knew that!: remembering life's lessons from Proverbs / Mike Root.
    p. cm.
Includes bibliographical references.
  ISBN 1-892435-36-5 (pbk.)
  1. Bible. O.T. Proverbs—Commentaries. I. Title.
  BS1465.53.r66 2003
  223'.706—dc21

2003006923

Dedication

This book is lovingly dedicated to Dean and Glenave Curtis, better known around the Root house as "Mamaw and Papaw." No one has ever had better in-laws than they have been to me. Their spirit of sacrifice, love, and hospitality has not only permeated our family, but touched thousands of lives—because that's how many people they've had in their home or assisted in some way. They are gentle, Christlike servants, who own the word "warm" when it's applied to "Warm welcome" and "Warm hearts." Thanks for your example, your support, and mostly for all you did in preparing an awesome wife for me. May your rolls never burn and may your beagles always find rabbits. I love you always.

Table of Contents

Introduction 9

Chapter One • "I Knew That!" 11

Chapter Two • "Use Your Head!" 29

Chapter Three • "Birds of a Feather" 41

Chapter Four • "Getting off Our High Horses" 57

Chapter Five • "Think Before You Speak" 73

Chapter Six • "Honesty Is the Best Policy" 89

Chapter Seven • "Don't Get Mad—Get Even!" 105

Chapter Eight • "Friends Are Friends Forever" 121

Chapter Nine • "Live One Day at a Time" 133

Chapter Ten • "Family Is Everything!" 141

About the Author 155

Introduction

I was late and I can't stand to be late! It wasn't that I'd overslept or been delayed by an unexpected phone call. It just took me longer than usual to do my morning jogging. When I got back to my house, I had forty minutes to get to a 9:00 A.M. staff meeting, and ten minutes of that time would be needed for the trip. I rushed through my shower, still perspiring as I toweled off; and the quick shave nearly took my lips and nose off with the whiskers. I dressed, jumped into the car, and drove like a madman with the AC blowing full blast to cool me off. It didn't help!

I pulled into the church parking lot with five minutes to spare and noticed one of my associate ministers leaving. How could he be leaving when there's a staff meeting in five minutes? As we pulled up next to each other and lowered our windows, he announced that he was on the way to the hospital to make a visit and I was welcome to come along if I wanted to. Just as the words "What about our Wednesday morning staff meeting?" were forming on my lips, the proverbial lightbulb clicked on and saved me from revealing my stupidity. It was Thursday!

I could blame it on the fact that I'd missed the staff meeting the day before while picking my wife up at the airport and Vacation Bible School replaced the usual Wednesday evening Bible classes that I taught. So it hadn't been a normal Wednesday with the normal routine, and I just lost track of which day it was. Somehow that didn't make me feel any less stupid.

I'm too young not to have my brain hitting on all cylinders! I'm just over the line on fifty, I have a wall full of diplomas, I've written four books, I preach for a large church with over a thousand members on the roll, and I'd like to believe that I'm analytical and quick thinking. On top of that, a doctor just declared me healthy, and, at one time, a counselor described me as very stable. How could I not know what day of the week it was?

It was a simple brain hiccup! A track skip! A glitch! We all have them and we all feel incredibly dumb when they happen. Maybe they are unconscious humility checks. Two by fours to knock us off our high horses and get us back down in the barn muck where we have a more balanced perspective of life. Who knows? The only thing that is for certain is they, like temptations, are "common to man." In fact, some of us have smacked our foreheads and said, "I knew that!" so many times that our skulls are taking on a Neanderthal look. I wonder if any of them ever ran into a saber-toothed tiger and said, "Now where did I leave that club?"

CHAPTER ONE
"I Knew That!"

COMMON SENSE GLITCH

While there are all kinds of reasons for mental lapses and forgetfulness, the garden variety, head-slapping "I knew that" is usually caused by one of the following. *The first cause for memory lapse is the **Common Sense Glitch**.* As the label indicates, this is when our common sense seems to temporarily check out for an indefinite time. Not only is this good for a serious head-slapping "I knew that," but it is usually good for a bruise, cut, shock, broken bone, burn, and a variety of much more serious things.

A few years ago, while bowhunting in northwestern Colorado, I had a serious common sense glitch. In the pre-dawn light, I was rushing to get into position on the side of a mountain where I could spot, and hopefully stalk, elk and mule deer as they came up the mountain from their nighttime feeding. I was in a hurry because I wanted to be in place before shooting light. Quickly moving through the sagebrush and scrub oaks, I suddenly came upon a patch of green grass covered with frost. I was surprised to see the frost so early in September, and I was thinking how pretty it looked as I stepped in the middle of it. Common sense? What happens when you step onto frosty grass on a mountain slope? Moments later, as I lay sprawled on the ground with a badly sprained knee, I thought, "I knew that! So why did I do it?"

There are many Bible characters who could be used to illustrate the common sense glitch, but for me there is one who truly stands out as the ultimate example. I am referring to Samson (Judges 14–16). I am sure that you remember him as a man of exceptional God-given strength and courage. His most memorable feat was the slaying of one thousand Philistines with the jawbone of a donkey (Judges 15:15). He was able to do this because "the Spirit of the Lord came upon him mightily" at the time. There were many times, however, when the Spirit of the Lord was clearly somewhere else.

I Knew That!

Early in the story of Samson we see him being tricked by his wife into telling the secret of his riddle. She promptly told the men with whom he had made the bet, and they claimed a victory that cost Samson thirty changes of clothing (Judges 14:12-20). On top of that, he lost his wife. One would think that he'd remember such treachery, but that is where his common sense glitch seemed to happen. Her name was Delilah.

He was in love and she was determined. The lords of the Philistines offered her a fortune if she would get him to tell her the secret of his strength and therefore help them to overpower him. She started to work on him and three different times he told her lies about the source of his strength and three times she tried to take his power away. Each time she had Philistine men waiting in the next room to subdue him once his strength was gone. Of course, since his answers were lies, nothing she tried worked; but she was clearly ruthless and relentless, and the Philistines were anxiously waiting for their opportunity. These are all indisputable facts that he must have known. Yet, "it came about when she pressed him daily with her words and urged him, that his soul was annoyed to death. So he told her. . . ." (Judges 16:16).

That was a serious common sense glitch. As a result, he suffered torture, ridicule, and imprisonment, and even though he took a lot of Philistines with him, it still cost him his life (Judges 16:18-31). Had he totally forgotten all the other attempts? Was he so cocky that he didn't care? Was he so overcome with her beauty and charm that he couldn't say no? She was about as subtle as a foghorn, yet he fell right into her hands.

FORGOTTEN FACTS

Another type of "I knew that" is **Forgotten Facts**. There are some things in life that are so true, so factual, that they become absolutes. In spite of their importance, we have a mental lapse and just forget about them. This is real forgetting too, not just rationalizing. For example, how many miracles had Peter witnessed and even participated in by the time of the famous last supper with Jesus? Dozens are recorded for us in the Bible, but John tells us that "many other signs" were performed by Jesus "in the presence of the disciples" besides the ones mentioned in Scripture (John 20:30). It is certainly safe to say that he had witnessed quite a number. He himself had walked on water with Jesus, and helped feed the five thousand with a little boy's lunch. He had dragged in the fish-filled nets, saw his mother-in-law healed, and heard Jesus calm the stormy sea. We'll never know how many things he witnessed and participated in during his three-plus years of following Jesus, but they were all things that clearly classify as unforgettable.

On top of all that, how many times had Jesus ever been wrong about anything He said? He couldn't be wrong! It was against His nature to be wrong! He was the Son of God and He was "the way, and the truth, and the life" (John 14:6). So how in the world could Peter have forgotten Jesus' prophecy that he would deny Him three times before the cock crowed the next morning? Maybe part of the hurt he later felt as he wept bitterly came from pounding his forehead and saying, "I knew that!"

We all know what it's like to just flat forget something. We were so excited when we moved to Texas in 1990 to begin a new work. One of the things we were most excited about was the opportunity to purchase our own house for the first time. It was a beautiful house too. In the dinning room and kitchen, our house had gorgeous lead crystal chandeliers that just sparkled with newness. The day we moved in, I was setting something down in the dinning room, and as I turned around I walked smack into the crystal chandelier cracking one of the beveled sections and putting a knot in my forehead. I felt incredibly stupid, but at least when I said, "I knew that," I didn't slap my forehead. I remembered I was already a knot-head. For the next eight years we lived in that house I had a cracked chandelier to remind me of one of my many moments of forgetfulness.

DISTRACTED

*Probably one of the most common types of "I knew that" is the **Distracted** type.* It's different from the Forgotten Facts type because this type isn't a matter of forgetting but of not seeing. Sometimes we get so distracted that we just don't pay attention to what we are really supposed to be doing. Have you ever missed your turn-off on the highway because you were really into something on the radio? Just the other day I shampooed my hair twice in the shower. It wasn't because my hair was that dirty. I was so lost in thought I couldn't remember doing it the first time. It's also why my skin looked like a prune and why all the hot water was gone.

How is it that a man who was described as "a man after God's own heart" could be so completely oblivious to his sins? Did David not realize that adultery, lying, and conspiracy to commit murder were sins? Yet there is nothing in the Bible that indicates he was aware of his sinful condition (2 Samuel 11). It wasn't until Nathan nailed him with "You are the man!" that he realized how distracted he had been (2 Samuel 12). Later, when he recorded his plea to God for a "clean heart," he declared, "For I know my transgressions, and my sin is ever before me" (Psalm 51:3). It's not hard to imagine him saying, "What was I thinking? I knew that!"

I Knew That!

We may not have a war to plan or a kingdom to run, but we get distracted and do things we shouldn't too. Maybe that is why Peter warned us to "Be on the alert. Your adversary, the devil, prowls around like a roaring lion, seeking someone to devour" (1 Peter 5:8). He's not going to be attacking when we're paying attention. He's waiting for us to get distracted. Then when he yells, "I got ya!" we'll be slapping our foreheads and yelling, "I knew that!"

LAZINESS

*Certainly one of the most frustrating and prevalent types of "I knew that" is the kind that springs from shear **Laziness**.* This type of head-slapping "I knew that" manifests itself in at least two forms. The first is procrastination, the putting off of things that really should be done now. I'm really bad about putting off things that I need to do, but I don't feel particularly motivated to do them. A good example is mowing the lawn. How many times have I put off mowing the lawn, rationalizing that one more day wouldn't make that much difference, only to have it rain the next day, or have some emergency come up and not have the time to do it? Then when I do crank up the mower, and begin fighting the taller, thicker grass, which requires more stops to empty the grass bag, and is a lot more work and takes a lot more time, I usually mumble to myself, "I knew that this would happen. Why didn't I do it when I was supposed to?"

The other prominent form of the Laziness "I knew that" is seen in the preoccupation with finding the easy way. OUCH! I have wasted more time trying to figure out the easy way to do some things than the time it would have taken just to do it in the first place. In my defense, there have been times when I was trying to find a better, more efficient way to do things, but many times it was for a less noble reason. Sometimes I wanted to impress others with my wisdom and insights; sometimes I just wanted to avoid looking like an idiot who didn't know the right way to do something; but most of the time is was simply an exercise in cutting corners.

It seems to me that Ananias and Sapphira might be good examples of this type of "I knew that." After all, they'd just seen how much attention Barnabas got for selling a tract of land and giving all of it to the Lord's work. What they did was simply find an easier way to get the same attention and at the same time, put some money in their pocket. There was no edict or command from the apostles that land profits had to totally be given to the Lord's work. It would have been fine for them to sell their land, give part of it, and keep the rest. It never was (and never will be) a matter of how much one gives, but that it be an act of compassion. By wanting everyone to believe they were giving all the proceeds from their land sale, they were destroying the very purpose of giving. For them, it wasn't an act of love, but a lie. It was easier to pretend like they gave it all than it was to give it all truthfully.

I suspect "I knew that" was seen in their eyes as Peter said, "Why is it that you have conceived this deed in your heart? You have not lied to men but to God." If they'd had time, I'm sure they would have slapped their head and said, "I knew that." Unfortunately, they ran out of breath first (Acts 5:1-11).

SMUG

*Maybe the worst kind of "I knew that" is the **Smug** type.* You're familiar with this one aren't you? It's when you hear something that from the tellers point of view is new, exciting, and important, but all you can say is "I knew that." It's not a statement of agreement as much as it is a self-inflating pronouncement that you are smarter, better, and way ahead of everyone else. Why do we feel the need to tell everyone "I've heard that joke before?" Is that important or germane to anything except boosting our egos? I suppose it's human nature to want to impress others with what we know, but isn't it something we grow out of eventually?

This becomes especially true when we make the commitment to walk by the Spirit and not by the flesh. There are at least two major reasons we can't afford to have this kind of "I knew that" in our life. First, it's a product of immaturity. All children feel the need to point out that they already know things. It's a matter of building self-esteem and a practical point of information because we don't know if they know things or not. As we grow up, we become secure enough that we don't have to inform others about our knowledge. It's assumed that adults are knowledgeable. To stress "I knew that" when no one cares or needs to know that you know is an exercise in selfishness, insecurity, and immaturity.

The second major reason we can't afford to have this kind of "I knew that" in our lives is pride. We will examine this in greater detail later in this book, but for right now it's sufficient to point out that "GOD IS OPPOSED TO THE PROUD, BUT GIVES GRACE TO THE HUMBLE" (James 4:6; 1 Peter 5:5). The proud person is not only cut off from grace, but God is against them. Wow! Not smart!

Remember the story of the rich young ruler in Luke 18? While we don't want to be to judgmental or harsh, doesn't it seem like he was a smug "I knew that" kind of guy? Yes, the point Jesus made was concerning the dangers of materialism, but don't you just hear the young guy saying, "I knew that" each time Jesus named off a command? "DO NOT COMMIT ADULTERY. DO NOT MURDER. DO NOT STEAL. DO NOT BEAR FALSE WITNESS. HONOR YOUR FATHER

AND MOTHER." Isn't his answer, "All these things I have kept from my youth," just another way of saying, "I knew that?" The only thing that surprised him was Jesus' command to sell all he had and follow Him. So he went away "very sad for he was extremely rich" and clearly loved wealth more than he did God. Maybe he was also sad because he was convicted about his selfishness by Jesus and now, in humility, he had to confess, "I knew that" (Luke 18:18-23).

Being smug about religious matters is simply being self-righteous like the Pharisees of Jesus' day. These were the ones that Jesus denounced and condemned as hypocrites, blind guides, fools, and whitewashed tombs (Matthew 23:1-36). Because they were very smug know-it-alls, they refused to listen to Jesus. Therefore, we find in the Bible one of the great ironies of history. The only people Jesus ever condemned in His three-plus years of ministry were the religious leaders of the day. They were the ones who, in their own minds, had their religious acts together; the ones who should have recognized who He was; and the ones who conspired to have Him put to death. I have a sneaky suspicion that when they received word that His tomb was empty, some of them quoted from the prophets and smugly declared, "I knew that."

SMART AND SMARTER

The reasons we might say, "I knew that" are endless. Most of the reasons tend to point out how fallible we are. Even the best and brightest among us will occasionally have a lapse in common sense, be forgetful, become distracted, procrastinate, seek the easy way, and we all occasionally get a little smug about how smart we've become. All of these can and should be humbling experiences through which we can grow and learn how to be better people—better servants of God. Just the process of writing this chapter has made me feel a lot dumber than I was when I started. I didn't have any problem coming up with personal illustrations for nearly every type of "I knew that." In fact, I had plenty to choose from. My self-esteem is not shattered, however, because I know that all of us struggle with trying to learn lessons that seem to need learning over and over again.

The challenge for us is to remember the lessons and avoid making the mistakes. "I knew that" is just retrospective revelation, or learning after the fact as we look back. Wisdom is learning ahead of time, or at least learning the first time so lessons won't be repeated time and again. Maybe the best kind of wisdom is to learn from someone else's mistakes. We do it all the time and feel so much smarter for it. An obvious example of this, that we all experience on nearly a daily basis, is driving our vehicles on the roadways. How

I Knew That!

often do you see the car in front of you hit a bone-jarring pothole, thus giving you a warning that you dutifully heed? How many times have you been on the Interstate and seen the car in front of you swerve to avoid a huge chunk of truck retread, giving you the time simply to change lanes? Have you ever been cruising down the highway, exceeding the posted speed limit, and seen the brake lights on vehicles way ahead of you come on? What did you do? (Of course, real wisdom is obeying the law and never having to worry about that State Trooper over the next hill.)

What does it say about us if we see people do stupid things and we follow their example? For some reason we didn't pick up on the lesson. The bottom line is that slapping our forehead and saying, "I knew that" is a confession of ignorance or even something worse. If we learn something, know it and believe it, and still fail to do it, we are at best forgetful, and at worse rebellious. This is especially true when it comes to the weightier matters of life that God has directed us to give special attention to. The Bible is God's Word. It doesn't *contain* it—it is IT! There's not a thing in Scripture that we can afford to ignore, forget, or discard. I am not talking about etching laws in stone or mere memorizing, but rather capturing the spirit of God's will in our lives.

There are some things that because of their God-given priority in life, we can't just keep slapping our head and saying, "I knew that." I have this strange picture in my head: many of us standing before God at Judgment, sounding like Peter Falk in *Colombo*, saying, "Ah, ah, yes Lord, love you with all my heart, soul, mind, and strength. Ah yeah, I knew dat!"

There are loads of Scriptures that warn us of the dangers of not doing what we know. Two verses in particular seem to echo in my mind with regularity.

> *"Therefore, to one who knows the right thing to do, and does not do it, to him it is sin."*
> –James 4:17

> *"Not every one who says to Me, 'Lord, Lord,' will enter the kingdom of heaven; but he who does the will of My Father who is in heaven."*
> –Matthew 7:21

So the challenge is for us not just to "know," but to internalize the concepts and pursue implementation of them in our life. While motivation is a key factor in this, maybe the root of the problem is found in our attitude toward knowledge. Life is a never-ending process of inputting knowledge into our brains. Do we like it, pursue it, and apply it? Satan loves for us to believe

I Knew That!

that "Ignorance is bliss" because God has been saying from the beginning that ignorance is bad.

Before we examine some classic "I knew that" areas of life, let's review some things that God has to say about knowledge.

A WORD TO THE WISE

Do you love learning something new? Do you enjoy discovering jewels of enlightenment? I love being surprised by new insights. In fact, my favorite TV channel is The Discovery Channel. I enjoy all the educational programs that are available now. I rarely watch the major network programs with all their silly sitcoms. Give me The Learning Channel, The History Channel, or A&E (Arts and Entertainment). My kids make fun of me and generally moan when I gain possession of the TV controls, but I like educational television, and that's what I want to watch. (Besides that, it's my TV and I'm still bigger than they are!)

I love it when something on one of these educational programs grabs my brain and makes me think. That's when your eyebrows rise and you say, "I didn't know that!" The other day I was watching The Discovery Channel program called *Investigative Reports*. The program was about women being victims of crime. At one point the narrator made the point that more women are victims of physical abuse from their husbands than all muggings, robberies, and assaults combined. That just struck me as incredible. Who would have thought that spousal abuse was so high? I sure didn't, and it really gave me something to think about.

Not long ago there was a program on The History Channel about the World War II war criminal Adolf Eichman. It covered the search for him and how they captured him in South America and put him on trial in Israel. I'm a history nut and I also remember seeing parts of the trial on TV when I was a youngster. I was very familiar with his involvement in the Holocaust, and all the terrible things he did during that dark period of history. He was found guilty of unbelievable atrocities. What I hadn't been aware of was one of the little ironies involved in his punishment. Eichman was executed by hanging, which I knew, but I didn't realize that his body was cremated afterwards. Instead of being honored with a grave and monument, he was treated like the millions of Jews he sent to the gas chambers. That really struck me as an interesting piece of historical trivia.

I was attending a lectureship at Pepperdine University a few years ago, and enjoyed listening to several speakers speak on the book of Philippians. Hey—I'm not exactly ignorant of Philippians! It's one of my favorite books of the Bible to study and preach on. So I didn't feel like I needed to take notes. Then one of the speakers made a statement that sent me scurrying for a pen and paper, and more importantly, my Bible. He said that even though the Book of Philippians is called "the Book of Joy" the word "joy" in the book is never used to indicate something they had. "What?" I thought. "This has to be blasphemy! The word 'joy' and 'rejoice' are in there too many times for that to be true." I quickly read through the entire book, and sure enough, Paul never describes the Philippians themselves as having joy. He talks about his joy, their need for joy and their sharing it when they get it, but never about them having it then. That may not seem earth shattering to you, but it at least changes the way we view Paul's letter to the Philippian church. Maybe he talked so much about joy because it was something they needed to develop rather than something they had in abundance.

I share these three short illustrations to simply show how and when learning is fun for me. These were thought provoking and interesting even though boarder-line trivia. It's somewhat hard to be fifty something and find huge new things to learn. It's the little new things that we must glean and reap wherever we can.

How do you feel about learning? Do you enjoy gaining new knowledge and insights into life? Is the process of discovery something that excites you? Does it drive you crazy not knowing the answer to a question or problem? Do you love being challenged to think, to study, or to solve a dilemma? Do you go out of your way to be taught something new? How many books do you read each year? How many seminars, lectureships, and workshops do you plan to attend this coming year? Do you feel like the "Old Dog" who can't be taught a new trick? Would you describe yourself as being "blissfully ignorant"?

One of the most amazing and sad things that I have seen a lot in my quarter-century of ministry is Christians who've stopped learning. I'm not talking about head-slapping "I knew that" stuff, but the pure absence of learning. I've known dozens of church leaders who haven't read a book, traveled to a special event, or had a new thought in decades. Their Bibles have more wear and tear from being picked up by the church janitor than because of their intensive study habits. Their Bible classes are boring, their minds are closed, and their leadership is uninspiring.

How can a child of God stop learning? We have all been called to "grow in the grace and knowledge of our Lord and Savior Jesus Christ" (2 Peter 3:18). The Christian life is a process that never stops. We don't just read the Bible, we examine "the Scriptures daily," handle "accurately . . . the word of truth," and know "the sacred writings which are able to give [us] the wisdom that leads to salvation through faith which is in Christ Jesus" (Acts 17:11; 2 Timothy 2:15; 3:15). Christians are into the Word of God! We "hunger and thirst" after it, we walk in it, we meditate on it; it dwells in our hearts "richly," and we love it! Since it is the words of Christ, it becomes the Bread of life to sustain us, the Truth that sets us free, and the Light that guides us.

How can we change without learning what we are to change to, and how we are suppose to do it? Make no mistake about it; we are constantly in a state of change. The word "change" may be anathema to some, but it is clearly a major theme of the New Testament. Listen to Paul's description of this change in 2 Corinthians 3:18: "But we all, with unveiled face, beholding as in a mirror the glory of the Lord, are being transformed into the same image from glory to glory, just as from the Lord, the Spirit." In Romans 12:2, he said that we are being "transformed by the renewing" of our minds, so that we can "prove what the will of God is." In Philippians 2:5, he simply tells us to have the same attitude or mind-set as Jesus. There are scores of verses that tell us to be "like" Jesus, or do things "as" Jesus would. In fact, a major theme of nearly every one of Paul's epistles is the simple plea to not be like we used to be. We're different now—changed because of Jesus!

I hope the point I am trying to make is obvious. Knowledge is important, but it becomes meaningless if we don't have the right attitude about it. If we don't want it, we won't seek it; if we don't care about it, it won't stick; and if we don't treasure it, it won't shine in our lives.

THE "I KNEW THAT!" BOOK

I wonder how many times Solomon said, "I knew that!"? It seems to me that his book Ecclesiastes is a portrait of forgotten values. Wasn't he given wisdom from God at the beginning of his reign as king? Remember the story from 1 Kings 3? God appeared to him in a dream and told him to "Ask what you wish me to give you." He could have asked for riches, a long life, or victory over all his enemies, but instead, he asked for an "understanding heart to judge Your people to discern between good and evil." God was so pleased with his choice that he gave him the first three as a bonus. God said, "Behold, I have given you a wise and discerning heart, so that there has been no one like you before you, nor shall one like you arise after you" (vv. 5-14).

So how could a guy who had so much God-given wisdom forget so much? Didn't he know before he pursued it that intellectualism, hedonism, materialism, egotism, and authoritarianism were all "vanity and striving after wind?" During all those years of experimenting and discovering what he had always known to be true, did he slap his head and say, "I knew that"? He ended his book with "The conclusion, when all has been heard, is: fear God and keep His commandments, because this applies to every person" (Ecclesiastes 12:13). Did he not know that at the beginning of his reign as king? You know he did because he received wisdom from God. He's the ultimate "I knew that" guy!

It's somewhat ironic that Solomon's writings in the Old Testament are part of what we call Wisdom Literature. They are a compilation of wise teachings from a man who couldn't seem to remember the wise thing to do. Nevertheless, remember what I said earlier about real wisdom being our ability to learn from others mistakes? That's why the Holy Spirit led Solomon to write Proverbs and Ecclesiastes. So that we could learn from his mistakes—so that we could learn from the ultimate "I knew that" man and save our heads from some slaps in the future. If Ecclesiastes is the "I knew that" book, then I suggest that Proverbs is the "Learn it right the first time" book. It teaches us what to know and how to know, and is an invaluable weapon in the war against selective memory.

A proverb is simply a jewel of knowledge from God's treasury of life. Solomon says they are important and useful for several reasons. He gives us a list at the beginning of his book.

> *To know wisdom and instruction*
> *To discern the sayings of understanding. . . .*
> —Proverbs 1:2

Every fall, hundreds of thousands of hunters across America head for the woods in pursuit of the elusive deer. One would think with that many hunters afield the deer population would be decimated, but that is not the case. In fact, the deer herd in America is larger now than it has ever been in the history of our nation. On the average, only one in ten hunters will harvest a deer in any given season. Why do so many fail to add venison to their family's freezer? Some are not very persistent or dedicated, but the biggest reason most don't succeed is because they grab their gun or bow, head for the woods, and simply plop down somewhere hoping to see some game. They ignore a primary rule of hunting: If you are going to hunt deer, you have to go where the deer are. Just because you are in the woods doesn't mean they are in the woods.

The same thing is true when it comes to finding wisdom. If you want it, you have to go to where it can be found. Just as it takes skills to scout and know where deer are going to be, it takes skill to find the right kind of knowledge. In fact, the word used here for wisdom (*hokmah*) is a Hebrew word for "skill." It is the same word used to describe the "skill of the craftsmen who worked in the tabernacle (Exodus 31:6), the 'wits' of seasoned mariners (Psalm 107:27), administrative abilities (1 Kings 3:28), and the 'wise advice' of a counselor (2 Sam 20:22).[1] "To know wisdom" means literally to acquire skills. One of the purposes of a proverb is to help us attain the skills we need to live for God. Thus Proverbs is the right place to find insights for living.

When we combine this with the call "to discern" or distinguish between things, to compare and evaluate what we hear and see, it seems clear that we need to be picky about what kind of knowledge we receive. You say, "Wait a second? Wisdom is wisdom. It comes from what is wise." That is true, but wisdom is only as good as the foundation or values upon which it is based.

In his epistle James wrote:

> *Who among you is wise and understanding? Let him show by his good behavior his deeds in the gentleness of wisdom. But if you have bitter jealousy and selfish ambition in your heart, do not be arrogant and so lie against the truth. This wisdom is not that which comes down from above, but is* **earthly, natural, demonic.** *For where jealousy and selfish ambition exist, there is disorder and every evil thing. But wisdom from* **above is first pure, then peaceable, gentle, reasonable, full of mercy and good fruits, unwavering, without hypocrisy.*
>
> –James 3:13-17, emphasis added

James clearly describes two types of wisdom that come from totally contrasting value systems. One is from God and is based on godly qualities, while the other is worldly with a selfish and sinful source. Paul simplified the two different types of wisdom when he wrote, "For since in the wisdom of God the world through its wisdom did not come to know God, God was well-pleased through the foolishness of the message preached to save those who believe" (1 Corinthians 1:21). So there is worldly wisdom and godly wisdom, and Paul declared, ". . . my message and my preaching were not in persuasive words of wisdom, but in demonstration of the Spirit and of power, so that your faith should not rest on the wisdom of men, but on the power of God." Then he added, ". . . we speak God's wisdom. . . ." (1 Corinthians 2:4-5,7).

In the introductory verses to Proverbs the writer is telling us that Proverbs will help us distinguish what kind of wisdom is profitable and from God. The Proverbs are from God and help us understand that the world's values are twisted, selfish, and based on the desire for immediate gratification. It gives us insights that we must have if we want to please God.

> *To receive instruction in wise behavior,*
> *Righteousness, justice, and equity. . . .*
> —Proverbs 1:3

Any book that can help us live wise or prudent lives is one we need to study regularly. "Wise behavior" is behavior that has been thought through. It is literally the opposite of stupid or thoughtless behavior. How much pain could we all have been saved throughout life if we'd only taken the time to think before we acted? How many head-slapping "I knew that's" could we have avoided? Proverbs is a book that will give us instructions on how to keep from doing something stupid. I should have read Proverbs back in the fourth grade when I decided that school was playtime and it cost me an extra year. I needed to read it back during my sophomore year in high school when I tried to run away and become a crew member on an ocean freighter. What a stupid idea that was! And then there was the time . . . well, you get the idea. We all have a boatload of experiences that we're not particularly proud of because they were, to put it kindly, unwise. Proverbs is our "How to" book for those of us who need wisdom—and who doesn't?

Wise or circumspect behavior means that we are going to do what is right, just, and fair. So Proverbs will guide us on our journey and help us stay committed to our covenant relationship with God, and make prudent decisions that are free from prejudice and bias. The three words "righteousness, justice, and equity" are words that, in Solomon's day, carried connotations that we probably don't associate with them today. Righteousness was not only doing right, but also primarily doing right for those who were unfortunate, poor, needy, or outcast. It was the "haves" taking care of the "have nots." Justice and fairness are key themes throughout the Prophets as those with wealth are condemned for ignoring and even abusing the poor, the widows, the orphans, and the sick.

Solomon seems to be saying that wise behavior is choosing to be godly, compassionate, and caring. Wouldn't you say that all the people who have helped you through the years were wise? Didn't they do the smart thing by assisting you? Being compassionate is always smart because compassion is godly, and it's always smart to be godly. The world doesn't understand that, but then that's why God's wisdom and worldly wisdom are diametrically opposed to one another.

I Knew That!

> *To give prudence to the naive,*
> *To the youth knowledge and discretion. . . .*
> —Proverbs 1:4

It's tough being naive. It's not only being unenlightened, it's inexperienced, uneducated, and out of touch. There are plenty of things about which we all can't say, "been there, done that," but we still understand and know about them. That's not the way it is with the naive. The naive are gullible and prime candidates for cons, jokesters, and evil teachers. They don't know what to believe, so they are open to be roped into anything.

The first shooting I ever saw as a police chaplain involved a hostage situation where a man was threatening to shoot his girlfriend if the police didn't leave. After a lot of negotiating, the girl was able to get out of the apartment where she was being held. The problem then became what to do about a drunken guy with a gun in his hands. He made the decision for us. He stepped out of the front door and fired twice at us. A plain-clothes detective, who was squatting down behind a tree just in front of the apartment, fired one shot, hitting the man in the upper thigh and knocking him to the ground. They then cuffed him and the medics bandaged him up for the trip to the hospital.

The next day at the police station I commented on what a great shot the officer had made, hitting the guy in the leg and taking him out without killing him. The other officers looked at me like I was some kind of idiot. They quickly told me that he had made a terrible shot, would probably be disciplined for it, and would certainly have to spend extra time at the shooting range. What I didn't know, because my knowledge of police work came from TV, was that they are trained to shoot to stop. That means they only shoot for the upper chest, never to wound or kill, but to stop. If the person shot lives or dies, that's beside the point. The shot in the leg was horrible not heroic. How was I to know? I was naive no longer!

In the world of archery there are plenty of awards and rewards if you compete in target or 3-D competition locally or right on up to the national level. Most of us, however, shoot bows and arrows for the shear challenge of it, and we target shoot just to get ready for bowhunting season. There is one achievement that we all like to accomplish occasionally, and that's to get a Robin Hood. A Robin Hood is when you make a perfect second shot right into the back of your first arrow, just like Robin Hood did in the movies. The difference is that these are aluminum arrows not wooden, and the shot must be even more perfect to split the nock and drive into the first shaft.

The first time I got a Robin Hood, I was shooting at an indoor archery

I Knew That!

range in Texas that was owned by a guy with whom I'd become a good friend. He was an expert in everything having to do with archery and bowhunting. So naturally I took my Robin Hood arrows over to him to show him how well I'd done, and to receive the appropriate strokes and such. He did praise my shooting and then he told me, "Ya know, if you'll call the company that makes those arrows and tell them you got a Robin Hood, they'll send you a dozen arrows free as a reward." Well, I was astounded and excited. A dozen arrows cost about fifty dollars and to get them free, in honor of my good shooting, was incredible. A few minutes later, after letting my ego swell sufficiently, he told me that he'd just been joking about the free arrows. I felt really stupid to have swallowed his bait "hook, line, and sinker." But then, how was I to know. I was new at all this.

The purpose of Proverbs is to give the naive, the young and inexperienced, the knowledge they need to avoid the traps of life. There's nothing wrong with being naive, but we don't need to stay that way. And there is nothing that says we have to experience things to learn about them. As mentioned already, real wisdom is learning from others' mistakes. Proverbs is the sage advice of the old warrior to the young recruit. It's the Spirit-filled reflections of the older and wiser saying, "Been there. Done that. So listen to me."

> *A wise man will hear and increase in learning,*
> *And a man of understanding will acquire wise counsel,*
> *To understand a proverb and a figure,*
> *The words of the wise and riddles. . . .*
> —Proverbs 1:5-6

Proverbs is not just for the naive. Any and every person who wants to learn, grow, and improve, will want to spend time with these words of wisdom. I love the emphatic tone of this passage. The phrase "A wise man **will hear**" is itself a concept worth memorializing on plaques and in framed, picturesque wall hangings seen at craft shows. It might not be a bad idea to put it on a poster and hang it in our church auditoriums too. Not just to encourage paying attention to the sermon, but to extol the virtue of listening. So often we seem to have more folks at church with hard heads than with open hearts. We have folks who glory in the saying, "You can't teach an old dog new tricks." It's probably the only time people enjoy being identified with a dog. God says that *wise people hear*, they listen and "increase in learning." What a novel idea!

Too many things at church are settled by comments like, "We've never done it that way before," or "Who knows what this will lead too?" I am particularly fascinated when I hear the not-so-sage advice that begins with, "It says in the Bible somewhere. . . ." It's sad when we have just enough knowledge to reveal to others how much we *don't* know! Our wisdom may really come from Hallmark rather than the Holy Book.

We know what we know and no one will make us know what we don't want to know. Whatever happened to lovingly, kindly, patiently, thoughtfully listening to what others have to say before we kill the discussion?

The wise person listens and tries to understand. He doesn't prepare his rebuttal while listening, nor does he pretend to pay attention just to patronize others. He may even restate what was spoken just to make sure that he understands what was said. His open heart is not threatened by new ideas, but rather filled with joy at the prospect of learning and growing. In fact, he seeks understanding and "will acquire wise counsel." That requires patience, humility, and a hunger for knowledge. We don't listen because we don't want to give it the time and effort; we are too proud to think we don't know something or might be wrong about what we do know; and we are self-satisfied with our present knowledge and have no appetite for more. That's not wise!

You're reading this, so you are probably not the closed-minded type. Don't you love being around people who want to learn and grow? I'm in the teaching business, teaching the most important message ever shared—the gospel, and there is nothing more thrilling than to share things with folks who really want it! It makes my heart sing to see the shining and alert faces of young people who are eager to drink in whatever the teacher has to say. And it's humbling to look out at a Sunday morning audience and see the smile-creased face of an elderly Christian, who is soaking up my message like she's never heard one before in her life. It brings tears to my eyes to have one of my shepherds come up to me and say, "You really made me think today." Not because of what it says about me, but because here's a man who was walking with God when I was a baby, and he still wants to learn and grow. He's a man of wisdom and understanding.

Do you want to understand a proverb, a figure, or a riddle? If you do, you may have to let someone help you. It may be a teacher, a professor, a tape, or a book, but if you're willing to listen and learn, to "acquire wise counsel," you'll not only understand, but also you'll be the one that others will be listening to.

I **REALLY** KNEW THAT!

So what if it's not all new! What's wrong with being reminded about things we already know? Repetition is the meat and potatoes of learning. We've all forgotten more than we've remembered. Sometimes repetition is

I Knew That!

fun. It makes us feel smart, secure, and ready for *Jeopardy*. We can smile and say, "I knew that!" Sometimes repetition is tedious, and we see it as old stuff, that is boring, and we smugly say, "Oh, I knew that." And then there's the time when repetition is convicting. We realize that we've forgotten something or been reminded of our shortcomings. That's when we hang our heads and whisper, "Yes, I knew that."

Was the rich young ruler really surprised with a totally new idea when Jesus told him to "sell all that you possess, and distribute it to the poor, and you shall have treasure in heaven; and come follow Me?" Was he that out of touch with Jesus and what He had been teaching, or was he hoping to be accepted because of what he remembered and knew, not by what he'd forgotten and ignored? "He became very sad; for he was extremely rich," but also because he'd been convicted by something that wasn't so new (Luke 18:18-24).

NOTE
1. "Proverbs," *The Expositor's Bible Commentary*, vol. 5 (Grand Rapids: Zondervan, 1991), pp. 904-905.

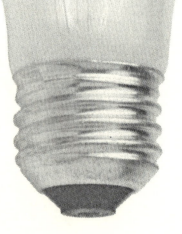

CHAPTER TWO
"Use Your Head!"

It's hard to think first thing in the morning. A good cup of coffee and a few minutes with *CNN Headline News* to make sure we're not at war, and I'm ready to exercise some brain cells. We all have times when we really don't want to think. We just want to put the brain on cruise control and "veg out" for awhile. But then there are the times when we need to think, and we discover that the old cerebellum is on strike—refusing to work. We may be exhausted, hungry, or on Nyquil; but whatever the cause, it's like trying to vacuum with an unplugged vacuum cleaner—there's motion but not much production.

Sometimes the mental gears are just not all clicking. We're awake, we're thinking, but we're just not running like a finely tuned machine. That's when you're liable to hear the age-old criticism that nearly all kids, especially sons, hear from their dads periodically. "Use your head!" Maybe your dad added ". . . for more than just a hat-rack." Of course, adults would never add that phrase when talking to another adult—would they?

It's been a long time since someone said that to me, but I've felt it. Haven't you? It's usually an auto mechanic's arched eyebrow after I explain what's wrong with my car. Or it's in the tone of the plumber's voice when he asks, "Did you try to snake out this drain yourself?" Then there's the cute little bank teller who says, "Sir, you forgot to carry the one over to the next number." Okay—so I'm not a mechanic, a plumber, or an accountant! I'm a preacher. Which reminds me of the time I mentioned a raise to my elders, and they said, **"You want what?"** What was I thinking!

None of us are sharp as a tack all the time. Even tacks get dull, and besides, they permanently have more flat area than sharp. Nevertheless, it's humiliating to have someone point out our mental deficiencies, though few they may be. What makes it even more frustrating and painful is that in nearly every case, when we've had one of these brief brain breaks, we find ourselves saying, "I

I Knew That!

knew that." But what good is it to know something if we don't remember to use it? It reminds me of a contemporary proverb I heard a while back: "The wise carry their knowledge as they do their watch—not for display, but for their own use." I like that. Especially since I have a Timex instead of a Rolex. The point is clear. To say, "I knew that" about something we've forgotten or haven't done is like saying I have a watch but I don't know what time it is.

So you don't have a photographic memory or total recall, and it's true that everyone forgets things every now and then. Are there some things that are so important that we just can't afford to forget them? You know that's true or you wouldn't be reading this book. The answer to that begins and ends with one word, God. (I hope you're saying, "I knew that!")

SOLOMON SAYS, "USE YOUR HEAD"

A motto is "a word, phrase, or sentence inscribed on something, as expressive of its character; a maxim adopted as a principle of behavior."[1] In the Boy Scouts it's "Be Prepared," in the Marines it's "Semper Fi," and at West Point Military Academy it's "Duty, Honor, Country." When I was attending Harding University, in the dark ages when it was still Harding College, the motto was "Educating for Eternity." I always thought that was a wonderful motto for a Christian school to have.

In Proverbs 1:7, Solomon said, "The fear of the LORD is the beginning of knowledge." That may be the most well-known verse in the entire book, and it should be. I have always thought of it as the motto of Proverbs. Proverbs 1:7 is to the Old Testament what John 3:16 is to the New Testament. It's central, pivotal, foundational, and sweeping in its application. It speaks to our character and certainly describes a principle of behavior that, at least initially, is *The* principle of behavior.

Let's look at the entire verse:

> *The fear of the* LORD *is the beginning of knowledge;*
> *Fools despise wisdom and instruction.*

This is serious "use your head" stuff! It's a call from the Holy Spirit for us to recognize what is really important. It seems to me that there are three primary elements in this verse: fear, facts, and fools.

FEAR

There's no telling how much of our life is spent in the grip of fear. Just think of all the decisions you've made throughout your life that were guided or influenced by fear. How many things did you not do because of fear? It may have been fear of rejection, or failure, or pain, or any one of a hundred other fearful things, but you decided to avoid it rather than deal with it. Things you didn't "try out" for, compete in, run for, participate in, work on, or join. What about the people you didn't get to know, the girls (or guys) you didn't date, and the career you could have had? And what about the things you didn't wear, the beards you didn't grow, the books you didn't write, the class you didn't teach, and the things you should have said to those who needed to hear them?

We are accustomed to operating out of fear. It's part of our life. We're afraid of being misjudged, misunderstood, or being left out. We fear being seen as afraid, or weak, or stupid. There is no telling what a man might do if his masculinity is threatened, or what some woman might do to show she's his equal. The list of examples is endless, but most of all they are all senseless. We fear everything and everyone except the One we should fear—God!

Jesus warned us not to fear man, who can only kill the body, but "rather fear Him who is able to destroy both soul and body in hell" (Matthew 10:28). Isn't it ironic that we spend our lives fearing man's ability to hurt us physically and emotionally, when God is the only One we need to be concerned with? When we learn to fear only Him, He literally gives us the ultimate freedom. It's freedom from man's threats, intimidation, acceptance, or rejection, and, for that matter, any evaluation they may have of us. He empowers us to truly live! Can you imagine what life would be like if our greatest passion were to please Him? When Solomon tells us that fearing God is the beginning of knowledge, he's not just giving us an intellectual principle of learning, but the secret to life, liberty, and the pursuit of happiness. (And all this time you thought that's what the *Declaration of Independence* did for us!)

So what does it mean to "fear God?" It's important that we not get too focused on our own mental pictures of fear. We fear crooks, bullies, and cops because they're big, tough, and in control. While it's true that God is big, tough, and in control, our fear of Him must be more than intimidation.

The Hebrew word that is used in Proverbs 1:7 has multiple meanings. It's the word that is used to describe the dread that the children of Israel felt in their hearts when they heard the report of the twelve spies about the promised land having fortified cities and giant warriors (Deuteronomy 1:29). The same word is translated as "frightened" when talking about the men on Jonah's boat after he told them he was fleeing from God (Jonah 1:10). It also means "to stand in awe," like the people did when Solomon showed such wisdom in judging between the two mothers who claimed the same baby (1 Kings 3:28). It is also translated "reverence," as in Leviticus 19:3 when everyone is commanded to "reverence his mother and his father."[2]

Thus we have a word that seems paradoxical. Fear of God includes both a cowering in fright and a drawing near in awe; a paralyzing dread, and a motivating reverence. It's a fearful submission, but it's also a longing to know personally. Our fear of God is softened by respect and admiration. We stand in awe of His power, yet we are incredibly impressed, and humbled, that He knows and cares about us.

Two images popped into my head as I reflected on this paradox. The first image was a memory of meeting a university professor that I truly respected and admired. I assumed he didn't know me from brother Adam. Indeed, I was somewhat intimidated to be in his presence. After introductions, the first comment he made was how much he enjoyed reading one of my books. Wow! The intimidation turned to warm appreciation, and a sense of self-worth flooded my body. Oddly enough, it was not ego inflating as much as it was humbling. So what kind of fear do we have when we discover that Almighty God, the Creator of all, really knows me and loves me?

The other image is of a small child tightly hugging his daddy's neck. He's four times as big as the child, strong enough to completely control the child, and far superior in intelligence. Is the child thinking of that? In a healthy family, is the child hugging daddy because he fears punishment if he doesn't? Of course not! The fear is there, somewhere in the conscious mind, but what's going on is love and "love casts out fear" (1 John 4:18). Maybe that's what we really mean when we talk about having "a childlike faith" in God. Fear must be there, but it's a special kind of fear that goes from the forefront to the rear as it is overshadowed by love.

FACTS

Knowledge is a means and an end, a process and a conclusion. The act of gaining knowledge becomes the gateway to gaining more knowledge. What we conclude and how we respond to knowledge, depends in large part on the premises, principles, and presuppositions we start with. For example, let's say three men are viewing the Hope Diamond, the world's largest blue diamond, which is on display in the Smithsonian Museum of Natural History in Washington, D.C. The first man looks at it with a quizzical expression on his face thinking, "How many billions of years did it take for this to evolve into such a beautiful stone?" The second man is also wide-eyed with awe, but he is thinking, "The God of heaven and earth created that glorious precious stone!" The third man, however, is musing, "What would really be incredible would be if I could figure out a way to steal that thing!"

Use Your Head!

One saw an evolutionary work of art, another an act of God, while the last guy was "casing the joint." Each one looked at the Hope Diamond with different eyes because they came from completely different starting points. Going forward with the facts depends on beginning with the right foundation, and the best foundation is "The fear of the Lord."

The fear of the Lord should be the first and dominant principle that guides all knowledge. Facts without fear leads to ultimate failure. The writer of Proverbs added another twist when he said, "The fear of the LORD is the beginning of wisdom" (9:10). Without a fear of the Lord, all knowledge and wisdom are suspect and maybe flawed. How many movies have you seen and how many books have you read where the existence of God is questioned, ignored, or maybe spoken of contemptuously. In most of today's entertainment, God is not exalted, He's blasphemed, which is incredibly odd in a nation that boasts "In God We Trust" and, in our Pledge of Allegiance, proclaim that we are "one nation" under Him.

Television is the worst offender, and I'm not just referring to the vulgar sitcoms and promiscuous primetime shows. Most of my favorite programs are on the education channels and they involve some kind of science like zoology, archaeology, oceanography, space, history, and the like. Unfortunately, nearly every program is predisposed to evolution or some other explanation for things besides the fact that God created them. I get very frustrated listening to their experts talk about animals having "perfectly evolved" to meet their environmental and survival needs, and it only took two million years. It's not just said occasionally, but over and over again, and it's always said as fact, rather than theory, even though it is *the theory of evolution* not the facts of evolution. These experts are essentially saying, "We don't know anything about this or how it happened, but we believe that it was a random natural selection that took millions of years." In my mind, that makes all of their expert commentary suspect. Without God in their explanations they have a flawed foundation.

The purpose of this book is not to deal with the existence of God. There are plenty of books on Christian Evidences if you want to study that subject, and if you never have, you should. God is—and that's a fact! The truth of that fact is the starting point for any area of knowledge we might seek to grow in and any kind of wisdom we might seek to have. At the same time we must understand that believing in and fearing God means more than obtaining knowledge and wisdom. After all, it is "the **beginning** of knowledge" not the whole enchilada. Because we fear God we understand where we came from and where we are going. He gives life, and He gives meaning and purpose to life. Solomon even said, "The fear of the LORD prolongs life, but the years of the wicked will be shortened" (Proverbs 10:27).

Another way to look at it is the reality that God not only gives meaning and purpose to life, but also meaning and purpose to death. He not only created our bodies, but also He created our souls, and it is His desire that our souls be with Him for eternity. There's more to life than living! There's the need to prepare for the time when flesh and blood becomes dust and ashes. We will live beyond the grave: ". . . it is appointed for men to die once and after this comes judgment" (Hebrews 9:27). That's a fact—get ready for it! The reality of that fact should change the way we look at everything, but especially death.

The fact of life after death is what made Paul declare, "For to me, to live is Christ and to die is gain. . . . I am hard-pressed from both directions, having the desire to depart and be with Christ, for that is very much better; yet to remain on in the flesh is more necessary for your sake" (Philippians 1:21-24). His knowledge of God was not a theory, but *fact*. This knowledge compelled him to live for Jesus and long to be with Jesus. It not only changed the way he lived but it changed the way he viewed death. I especially like the factual way he stated it in 1 Corinthians 15:50:

> *"Now I say this, brethren, that flesh and blood cannot inherit the kingdom of God; nor does the perishable inherit the imperishable."*

He always seemed to be saying, "Don't get too attached to that body of yours because it won't get you to heaven." Flesh and blood won't go to heaven because heaven is a spiritual realm where imperishable spirits live. We will be given a totally new body. We say we want to go to heaven, but we don't want to die to get there. Yet we must be changed from mortal to immortal and from perishable to imperishable, and this is a fact whether we die or are standing when the Lord returns. It's a fact whether we ignore it, dread it, or long for it.

That is why knowledge of facts must be combined with the right kind of motivation. According to all the surveys I've ever seen, the vast majority of Americans believe in the existence of God. But, if there is no fear of God, what good is it to believe in Him? I guess we could say that we couldn't even begin to know Him without fearing Him. If we don't know Him we can't understand why He made us, why He planned for our salvation before He even created the world, and why He loves us so much. If we don't really know Him we'll never understand His holiness, His mercy, and His gift of free choice. If we don't know Him we will never understand why Jesus died, and we will never really know Jesus.

Right about now you should be saying, "I knew that." Right? You know

Use Your Head!

the facts and you have the fear, so this is all old stuff to you—right? Well here's another twist. Solomon also said,

> "The fear of the LORD is to hate evil. . . ."
> –Proverbs 8:13

Did you know that? To fear God means that we must hate or despise evil! That's a fact about fearing God. We hate evil! That doesn't mean we play with it, get close to it, or we rationalize it. It means we detest it down deep where the feelings of hate usually come from. Ouch! I'm not there yet, are you? Maybe I don't fear the Lord as much as I thought I did.

FOOLS

When I was a kid we had a wide array of verbal weapons to use to put someone in his or her place. We had the usual "dummy" and "stupid," but we also had some creative tags to place on people. It was years before I discovered that the derogatory name "flick" was simply a derivative of the word afflicted. "Flick" was simply a crude way of saying that someone was mentally afflicted. You can probably figure out to what a "tard" or a "spaz" referred. During my college years we had a softer appellation to stick on someone in need of humbling. It was the term "Dilbert"; it was used as a synonym for dumb. During the last year and a half of college, I was a married man. We had a cat that did so many crazy things that elicited the epithet "Dilbert" that it stuck as a permanent name.

But, when I became an adult I put away childish things and started referring to others by their real labels—liberal, conservative, or progressive. (At times, I have been either all of these or none of these, depending on the standard being used at the moment, and to whom you were talking.)

Why do we feel the need to label or call people names? We don't have the right to judge, condemn, or belittle anyone! We are what we are by the grace of God and that grace was given to us to be given to others. If you want to talk names, God sent His Son to die for us while we where "helpless," "ungodly," "sinners," under "the wrath of God," and "enemies" (Romans 5:6-10). How is that for a list of names? If that doesn't create a humble and non-judgmental heart in us, nothing will.

Even Jesus pointed out that we have no business calling others names and harboring ill will in our hearts. He said that calling someone a "fool" could cause the caller to be lost in "hell of fire" (Matthew 5:21-22). First of all, we're not perfect ourselves, and secondly, we can never know what is going on in another person's heart. On the other hand, God is and God can!

That is why we must also give attention to the second part of Proverbs 1:7, "Fools despise wisdom and instruction." This is the antithesis of what he said in the first part of the verse. The person who wants to learn, grow, and draw close to God must begin by fearing Him. If someone doesn't want that, God says he's a fool. That's not my judgment but God's, and He's not just labeling or name calling, He's stating a fact. Just like the Psalmist said in Psalm 14:1, "The fool has said in his heart, 'There is no God.'" That's not an opinion. It's the all-knowing God who searches the hearts of men stating a truth.

That means every time one of those "experts" on one of the education channels spouts off about evolution being fact, he or she is simply revealing that he or she is a fool. And when you reach one of those dramatic moments in a movie when the hero shouts, "There is no God. How could He let something like this happen!" Keep it to yourself, but whisper, "Fool." And of course, when you find yourself doing something that you think God doesn't see or care about, don't forget to say—well, you know what.

The Hebrew word for "fools" is used to refer to "those who are thick-brained or stubborn."[3] Solomon had a great deal to say about fools. Pull out your concordance and see how many references to "fools" and various forms of the word there are in the book of Proverbs. While there are a lot of things said about them, the most condemning element of being a fool seems to be the shunning of any attempt to learn and grow. In the Hebrew poetry of Proverbs 1:7, Solomon is simply saying these people refuse to know God.

The fool despises wisdom. This is more than just a temporary case of intellectual burnout, or a need to take a break and relax awhile. To despise is to treat as worthless or contemptible. If someone despises wisdom, what's left but foolishness? It's one thing to be dumb but it's worse to chose to stay that way. How could someone literally despise wisdom?

This would be a great place to speak up for all the school teachers of the world who struggle with students who have so much potential but they just refuse to learn. I was one of those kids once, and I received the "you're not using you potential" speech several times. The teacher was right, but the problem wasn't despising wisdom. It was more a case of immaturity than rebellion, and the lack of enthusiasm was more a reflection on the methods and material than it was a refusal to learn. The wisdom and instruction being discussed by Solomon is knowledge about God and seeking a relationship with Him. If we don't want that, we are fools. To despise what's most important in life is foolish.

The Bible is filled with people who are good examples of despising wisdom and instruction. What about Pharaoh's refusal to let Moses lead the chil-

Use Your Head!

dren of Israel out of Egypt? How many signs, miracles, and plagues would you have to witness before you let God's will be done? And then to send your army into the Red Sea after them! That's truly a hard-core refusal to accept the great I AM. What about Jonah? Did he really think that God wouldn't notice his detour? Then there was Esau, who sold his birthright for a bowl of stew. Didn't that cheapen the value of what it meant to be the firstborn, and didn't it affect his relationship with God? What about Shimai cursing David and throwing stones at him? Did he miss the fact that David was God's anointed? Don't forget the hand-washing Pilate, the politician Caiaphas, and the worm-eaten Herod. These are all folks who either temporarily or permanently ignored God. A little bit of wisdom could have saved them all a lot of grief.

Our God is a loving and merciful God, but He doesn't accept foolishness as an excuse for disobedience. It seems to me that God is much more understanding, and indeed forgiving, of ignorance than He is of one who refuses wisdom and discipline. An excellent example of this is seen in the condemnation directed towards those who reject the obvious truth about God. In Romans 1, Paul is talking about those who were outside of a covenant relationship with God, but who still should have acknowledged Him as the one and only God. Paul declared:

> *For the wrath of God is revealed from heaven against all ungodliness and unrighteousness of men, who suppress the truth in unrighteousness, because that which is known about God is evident within them; for God made it evident to them. For since the creation of the world His invisible attributes, His eternal power and divine nature, have been clearly seen, being understood through what has been made, so that they are without excuse.*
>
> *For even though they knew God, they did not honor Him as God or give thanks, but they became futile in their speculations, and their foolish heart was darkened. Professing to be wise, they became fools, and exchanged the glory of the incorruptible God for an image in the form of corruptible man and of birds and four-footed animals and crawling creatures.*
>
> –Romans 1:18-23

The reality of the one true and living God is so obvious that to ignore or reject it is foolish. Knowledge of Him is "evident" within us, His nature and characteristics are "clearly seen," and His creation screams of His existence. To then reject all that and, in the name of intellectualism, bow down to some

I Knew That!

idol—some *thing*, is inexcusable and places one under the wrath of God! It is much wiser to have a fear of God to begin with than it is to suffer the wrath of God in the end! These people "knew God" but, because they didn't have the proper respect for Him, did not "honor Him as God, or give thanks." These foolish people didn't care about truth. As Paul said, "For they exchanged the truth of God for a lie, and worshiped and served the creature rather than the Creator, who is blessed forever. Amen" (v. 25).

Why is it that "The fool has said in his heart, there is no God"? What makes him a fool? He's lying and he knows it! It is my personal opinion that there is no such thing as an absolute, truthful atheist. People may do a pretty good job of suppressing what is in their hearts, and may be able to ignore what's there, but "God is evident within them; for God made it evident to them." There is an awareness of God that is instinctive just like survival is instinctive, and one must work to suppress either one. Just as we may replace our survival instincts with all the comforts and security of modern technology, we may replace our instinctive need to worship God with worship of self, but it doesn't totally remove the instinct. Ignoring or replacing God is simply a foolish attempt to escape responsibility and accountability for our life's choices—our sins. We are all congenital theists, and to say, "there is no God" is as foolish as saying, "there is no reason to live."

There is an element of irony in pointing out that "fools despise . . . discipline." Discipline means instruction or learning. If one decides to reject instruction, he never really rejects instruction, he is simply choosing one discipline over another. No one lives in a vacuum were there are no influences or options. Satan is alive and active, and his first line of battle is getting people to choose his will over God's will. When we say "no" to God, we are simply saying "yes" to Satan. He's got his own school of thought and he doesn't care who gets the credit for converts. It may be selfishness, materialism, greed, laziness, idolatry, or any number of alternate choices. As long as we don't choose God, he gets the victory.

That's why I say it's ironic. The fool thinks he or she is discounting wisdom and instruction, but all he or she is doing is exchanging God's truth for Satan's lie. They become not just fools, but Satan's fools! We all listen to someone. It's either the Evil One or the only One true and living God. That's a fact, and only a fool can't figure out which One is best.

FOOL FOOD

There's probably no one more foolish than someone who's in love. The word "infatuate" actually means "to make foolish."[4] Don't you have some memories from high school and college of doing totally crazy things because you thought you were in love? I remember spending money on gifts, traveling long distances, writing dozens of notes, letters, and even poems, listening to "our song" over and over, pining away the days when separated, and inscribing her name on everything I owned, (which always came back to haunt me when we broke up and I started dating another girl). Yes, I was foolish, but for a worthwhile reason, I thought. What still amazes me about that is I didn't care what anyone else thought about it! Who cares if they though I was crazy? I was in love!

In most situations, being a fool for the sake of love is totally different than being a fool for Satan. Paul talked about loving God so much that he didn't care that he became "a spectacle to the world." Doing God's work may at times look foolish to those who don't understand what it means to love Him with all our heart, soul, mind, and strength. It doesn't matter what others think if God is pleased with our obedience. That is why it's really an honor to be "fools for Christ's sake." The world may label us fools, but God has already declared who the real fools are (1 Corinthians 4:9-10).

Our life's pursuit is developing a relationship with God. We spend our lives getting to know Him and loving Him. The relationship may have to start with a healthy fear of His power and majesty, but He wants it to grow into a loving Father and child relationship. A relationship based on love.

It reminds me of one of my favorite Broadway and movie musicals, *The King and I*. You may remember, it's the story of a beautiful English girl who is hired to be a teacher for the children of a king. At first, she is overwhelmed by the culture and traditions of the small kingdom and its domineering king. In fact, she is quite intimidated by the king. The story is filled with clashes of priorities and perspectives between the king and the teacher, but gradually, the relationship grows, and intimidation is replaced by warmth and respect, and maybe even love. You probably remember one of the big hit songs that came from this musical; "Getting to Know You." It's a light, lovable, and happy song about a growing relationship.

Any relationship that is important and that we want to see grow, is a relationship that never stops the "Getting to Know You" process. We must never stop getting to know God. We must seek Him in every part of His creation. We must search His Word for understanding. We must learn more about Him as we see Him in the lives of His people. We must pray, because there is no relationship without communication. And while we must fear Him as God Almighty, we must embrace Him as the source of all love, grace, and forgiveness. Getting to know Him is not just a lifetime pursuit but an eternal quest.

I Knew That!

NOTES
1. *Webster's New World Dictionary of the American Language*, 1964, p. 489.
2. "Proverbs," *The Expositor's Bible Commentary*, vol. 5, p. 907.
3. Ibid.
4. *Webster's New World Dictionary*, p. 384.

CHAPTER THREE
"Birds of a Feather"

It's amazing how many sayings and clichés we have in our communication repertoire. It's nearly impossible for us to speak for very long without revealing a lot about ourselves through the clichés we use. I guess you might say we "spill the beans," or "let the cat out of the bag," or at the very least, "showed our hand." Sayings and clichés are incredible sociological identifiers. In other words, they reveal where we were "born and bred," where we "hang our hat," and what we do to "bring home the bread." They come from our families, our region, our education, our occupation, our entertainment, our religion, and anything else that has influenced us.

Personally, when I was knee-high to a grasshopper, we were so poor we couldn't pay attention. Since, "attitude determines altitude," and "the Lord helps those who help themselves," we picked ourselves up by our own bootstraps and made the best of a bad situation. Nobody promised us a rose garden and we didn't look at the world through rose-tinted glasses. We just grabbed the bull by the horns and turned the lemons into lemonade. Where we lived, on the poor side of town, crime was rampant in the streets. You couldn't swing a cat by the tail without hitting a crook. But when the going gets tough, the tough get going, so we bit the bullet and did what had to be done. I wasn't exactly an Einstein in school because a little knowledge is a dangerous thing. Nevertheless, I paid my dues, saluted the flag, marched to the right drumbeat, hit the books, burned the midnight oil, and I got to do the Pomp and Circumstance shuffle. All of life was ahead of me; I could reach for the stars, grab the golden ring, and climb every mountain. I had several life-changing events, the crowning moment of which was my decision to walk the walk and talk the talk of being a child of God. Now I preach the Word, keep the faith, let my light shine, give as I have prospered, pray for all those for whom it is my duty and privilege to pray for, and always remember that

I Knew That!

people don't care how much I know until they know how much I care. That's the whole enchilada, the whole nine yards, the nuts and bolts, from soup to nuts, from the word go, the big picture, the gory details, the bread and butter, meat and potatoes, and the whole truth and nothing but the truth.

That's just the tip of the iceberg or the hem of the garment, if you know what I mean. I don't remember where they came from. They're just part of my life. We pick up new ones all the time as we mix with new people or are in new environments. I have expressions, clichés, and colloquialisms from living in Virginia, Texas, Arkansas, Georgia, and now Tennessee. Some came from sports, some from my years with the police, some from church work, reading, and some are peculiar to my family. My family has so many inside jokes involving words and expressions that, at times, we almost have our own language.

Most of the more cultured or classical sayings and expressions I know I first heard from my mother. She was a very well-read, self-educated woman who never stopped learning her entire life. I have never known anyone who could do a crossword puzzle faster than she could. While I don't remember exactly when or where I first heard it, but I feel quite sure that she was the first person I heard say, "Birds of a feather flock together." It probably didn't make much of an impression on me at the time, but through the years it has been the source of many head-slapping "I knew that's."

THERE'S NO PLACE LIKE HOMOGENEOUS

On the surface, the truism "Birds of a feather flock together" seems like a rather elementary observation. While there are deep intellectual and metaphorical principles inherent in this aphorism, it is just as likely to elicit a profound "Duh!" from the rhetorically challenged. It is a thought-provoking observation. To put it another way, it's a zoological truth with sociological application. One could say that it refers to the psychological implications of homogeneous interaction resulting in cohesive habitation. Or you could just say that you're going to hang around with people who are like you.

I like being around people who are like me. After all, I like me, so why wouldn't I like people who are like me? It's really natural, even instinctive, for us to seek out others who are like us. The word homogeneous means being the same or having similar qualities or attributes, having things in common. We are drawn to people with whom we share things. The first order of business when we find ourselves spending time with someone is to determine how much we have in common with one another.

If we share things that are really important to us, the bond can be instantaneous. If you ever travel in a foreign country for a long period of time and happen to run into a fellow American, it's like finding a long-lost friend. If you met the same person in New York, you might not give her the time of day. When I lived in Texas I discovered that many Texans felt that way when they traveled to another state. Everywhere else was foreign, and if they ran into another Texan it was "old home week."

One of the things that I enjoyed during my police chaplain years was the incredible nationwide fraternity of police officers. Wherever I went, when a police officer there discovered that I was a police chaplain, we were sudden buddies. I had many wonderful friendships develop when they thought of me as "one of them." I'm ashamed to say that it even got me out of a speeding ticket once. On the positive side, however, I did get a first-class tour of the U.S. Capitol when the Capitol Police found out I was a badge-carrying member of "The Group."

I really enjoy finding fellow bowhunters. Because it is a very personal hobby, with serious challenges and few successes, most are pretty quiet about their interest in the sport. When I run into someone who is as enthused about it as I am, we tend to become friends rather quickly. Several of my fellow preachers are dedicated bowhunters, and we have a special bond that goes deeper than a shared vocation. Even when I've met total strangers on the other side of the country, when we discovered our mutual interest in hunting with archery, we became instant friends. Almost without exception, I have found serious bowhunters to be people of warmth and integrity.

Of course there is nothing like a shared faith in God. Meeting someone who loves the Lord like you do is one of the sweet joys of Christian living. "Birds of a feather flock together" is an appropriate metaphor to me because everywhere I go I look for brothers like a homing pigeon. I seek the fellowship of the saints before I seek anything else. I have found that God's people are wonderful whether I'm in California or Washington, D.C. I've been with some tremendously inspiring Christians in Holland, Germany, and even Saudi Arabia, where it's illegal to be a Christian unless you're there on a temporary work assignment with an oil company. I found godly people on the police force, the basketball court, the business world, and in book publishing (like the wonderful folks at Covenant). God's people are out there, and if you want to be with other heaven-bound family members, they're not hard to find.

The "Tie That Binds" us together in Christ is a special, beautiful, and powerful thing. It's not a shared hobby or a common vocation. It's a shared Lord, a shared faith, a shared hope, a shared salvation, a shared mission, and a shared destination. It's a bond that draws us together, tears down walls that divide, and makes us a family even when we are not related. It transcends all differences like race, status, or gender. As Paul put it:

> *For all of you who were baptized into Christ have clothed yourselves with Christ. There is neither Jew nor Greek, there is neither slave nor free man, there is neither male nor female; for you are all one in Christ Jesus.*
>
> –Galatians 3:27-28

Not only do "birds of a feather flock together," but sheep of The Shepherd flock together too. And I must say, while it's a great flock, He's an awesome Shepherd. (Check out Psalm 23 and see.)

DON'T BE A BIRD-BRAIN!

After taking you down that long road of explaining, illustrating, and applying the timeless saying "Birds of a feather flock together," I must point out that my mother wasn't sharing it with me as a jewel of sociological wisdom, but rather as a warning. If my memory serves me well, the times when my mother quoted this phrase were usually times when she was concerned about the kind of people I was spending time with. In Southeast Washington, D.C., in the late fifties and early sixties, there was a lot of street gang activity. Not only was I in one, but I was the leader of it. While the purpose of the gang was primarily for protection and not for criminal activities, there were several in our gang who were certified juvenile delinquents. She was trying to impress upon me that while we were flocking together and not totally "birds of a feather," that could change with continued association.

In looking back on those tough years in a tough part of town, there was never a time when I got in trouble on my own. Every time I found myself in serious trouble, it was because of my "friends." I wanted to impress them, or be accepted by them, so I did stupid things. Peer pressure! There were even a few times when I got in trouble just for being part of the group and not for anything that I specifically did. There were plenty of times when I smacked my forehead and said, "I knew this would happen!"

I had one particular friend that seemed to always get me in trouble. He, of course, thought I was the one who always got him in trouble. One day the school principal was giving us one of many lectures/warnings, and he said, "You two guys are like nitro and glycerin. When you are by yourself, you're harmless, but when you're put together you become nitroglycerin." We thought that was hilarious. We even started calling each other, Nitro and Glycerin. It was certainly more modern than Butch and Sundance. I don't think we would have made it out of adolescence alive if one of us hadn't moved to a different school.

All of us are influenced by the people we spend time with. That influence can be good or bad, depending on what kind of people they are and what kind of person we are. We may not start out being like them, but if we flock together with them, it could bring about a feather transformation.

Our brothers in Corinth seem to have had a very difficult time building flock cohesion. In his first letter to them, Paul reprimands them for being divisive about nearly everything. In fact, the entire letter is a plea for unity. They divided over who baptized them (chapters 1–4), they had lawsuits against one another (chapter 6), they were divided over food (chapter 8), over supporting Paul (chapter 9), and over spiritual gifts and assembly activities (chapters 10–14). In chapter 15 Paul tried to help them through what may have been their most serious problem, their inability to accept and understand the reality of the resurrection.

Paul offers several arguments and explanations for the resurrection. He basically says that because Jesus was raised from the dead we will be, too. It's God's plan and it will happen to everyone, even those who are alive when the Lord returns. Our bodies will be changed from physical to spiritual, mortal to immortal, perishable to imperishable, in an immeasurable instant of time. Death will be conquered and eternal life with God will begin. It's as much a fact as the life, ministry, death, and resurrection of Jesus.

Interestingly enough, one of the reasons they seemed to struggle with this fundamental doctrine of faith was the negative influence of others. Some of the philosophers of the day were teaching hedonism and were very much "anti-life after death." That is why Paul said, "If the dead are not raised, LET US EAT AND DRINK, FOR TOMORROW WE DIE" (v. 32). This was a reference to those who were teaching that there was no resurrection, and there were several. There line of reasoning simply said that since there was no resurrection, we should fulfill all our wants and desires.[1] Christians must not associate with those who teach such. Paul declares, "Do not be deceived: 'Bad company corrupts good morals.'" (v. 33). He used a quote from Greek literature to help make his point. "Bad company corrupts good morals" is from Menander's comedy, *Thais*, and was a relevant way to reinforce his warning.[2]

Be careful with whom you chose to hang around! They could influence you to change your values, priorities, and even your theology. When someone influences us to reject the reality of the resurrection, the ripple effect could not only involve a change of flocks, but the alienation of a soul.

Another example of flock avoidance is found in Proverbs 22. Most of us have never had to worry about someone influencing us to deny the resurrection, but we have probably been around someone who fits Solomon's warning in verses 24 and 25.

> *Do not associate with a man given to anger;*
> *Or go with a hot-tempered man,*
> *Or you learn his ways*
> *And find a snare for yourself.*

Many of us have struggled with controlling our tempers. In the earlier years of my life, I used to wonder if I'd ever get over the tendency I had of blowing-up so easily. There were times when I was the "man given to anger" that others needed to avoid. Through prayer and a lot of guidance from older Christians, and just plain old growing up, it became a much smaller problem. Today, I truly don't like to be around someone who is "given to anger." Some folks are like walking pressure cookers waiting to explode. We've even coined a whole new label for those who can't seem to control themselves while driving their motor vehicles. It's called Road Rage. I see it all the time in city driving as people are fighting heavy traffic and delays from construction and accidents. Unfortunately, we have to share the roads with these motorized maniacs. We don't have the luxury of not associating with them. Our real challenge is making sure we don't "learn his ways, and find a snare for yourself." I come nearer losing my cool in traffic because of inconsiderate and aggressive drivers than I do anywhere else in my life. I have simply decided that it's a wonderful opportunity to be Christlike.

There are people we can choose to avoid. People with short fuses who walk around with lit matches in their hands. An angry spirit is a hateful, bitter spirit. When I wrote this there was a criminal trial going on in Jasper, Texas. Three white men chained an innocent black man to the back of a truck and dragged him down an asphalt road, ripping his body apart, and killing him. It was a hate crime. A crime of anger-gone-to-seed. The first man being tried for the murder argued that he was influenced by the hate and anger of fellow prisoners during a previous incarceration in a Texas prison. He said that he learned racial hatred from the guys he hung around with. If that's true, not only did he make some seriously bad choices, but he found "a snare" for himself. He became like the flock he chose to roost with. Surely he hadn't always been a vulture.

Be careful who you hang with. You may be hanged together.

FLOCK FLIRTING

We are what we are today because of the many people who have influenced our lives. Sometimes we got to choose who would influence us, as we picked friends, joined clubs and organizations, and gave allegiance to certain philosophies, books, and entertainment. Other times we had influences placed on us whether we wanted them or not. We were born into a family, assigned teachers, and required to be part of some groups with members and leaders we simply had to accept. As we grew and as we learned right from wrong, the one thing we could always choose was whether or not we were going to be influenced by those people we were with. That was true whether the influence was for good or evil.

I witnessed an example of this many times when I was a police chaplain. Every rookie police officer was assigned to a Field Training Officer (FTO) the day they graduated from the academy. The FTO would be their immediate supervisor for their first year. I can't remember how long it was, but for a good bit of that time they had to ride with and be under the immediate supervision of their FTO before they were "cut loose" to patrol on their own. The FTO had more influence on that rookie than any other factor in all their training.

One of the FTOs at my station had absolutely no business being an FTO. He was everything that the department was trying to avoid. Modern cops have to be smart, polite, diplomatic, and very professional or they will not last long. In the old days, the cops were authoritarian, tough-guys, and often unaccountable. Now they have to be as much lawyers and social workers as "crime busters." This FTO was from the old days. His model was Dirty Harry or John Wayne, and he saw himself as the biggest and baddest guy on the street. His job was to be in charge, be boss, and intimidate the crooks (and citizens) into submission.

I watched him train two different rookies. Both were bright-eyed idealists, longing to make a difference in both fighting crime, and making the community a better place. They saw themselves as public servants. They were there to serve and protect, not to rule.

One went through the FTO period and became a completely different person. He was a clone of his FTO. He swaggered and talked tough. He complained about service calls and only wanted "real police" assignments. He liked to talk about the guys he clubbed, cars he chased, and crooks he "drew down on." He didn't care about people. He only cared about power.

The other rookie had the same FTO, but he was able to "pick the bones out of the fish." He learned what he needed to learn to be a good cop, but he refused to adopt the attitude and actions of the cowboy he had as an FTO.

I Knew That!

The last time I heard about him, he rose to be one of the top commanders in the department. The other officer quit after a few years and some high-level encouragement.

They were under the same influence, but one chose to accept the good *and* the bad, while the other only allowed the good or useful to be accepted. So it is possible to flock together without changing feathers, but it is, however, better to avoid those bad flocks entirely if you can.

If I knew who said it first I'd give him or her credit, but I like the saying I've seen on T-shirts and coffee mugs, "It's hard to soar with eagles when you're surrounded by turkeys." It's wonderfully apropos to our topic. Sometimes you want to flock together with eagles, but you find yourself in the middle of a flock of turkeys. (To all members of the National Wild Turkey Federation, this is a play on words and not meant to cast aspersions on this magnificent bird.)

It's rare that people desire to be pulled into evil. Some people are evil and they're looking for evil people to be with. Most, however, tend to be pulled into evil gradually. When Moses went up on the mountain to receive all of the Law from God, he received not only the Ten Commandments, but also all of the itemized laws of the old covenant. One of those laws was "You shall not follow the masses in doing evil" (Exodus 23:2). Yet, while he was up there getting these laws, the children of Israel where building and worshipping a golden calf.

As this story is recorded in Exodus 32, it looks as though Aaron, who had been left in charge by Moses, was intimidated and pushed into the whole thing by the people. The people assembled around him and demanded that he make them a god because they had lost their confidence in Moses ever coming back. He gave in and ordered the construction of the golden calf. When Moses returned, and in anger tossed the tablets to the ground, Aaron was quick to point out ". . . you know the people yourself, that they are prone to evil" (v. 22). Yet Moses knew "that the people were out of control—for Aaron had let them get out of control. . . ." (v. 25). In the movie version the ground opened up and swallowed the rebellious people, but the Bible says that Moses ordered the Levites to kill them with the sword. Nothing was done to Aaron. Maybe Moses recognized that he was weak and got pulled into it by the people. He didn't wake up one morning and say, "Let's commit idolatry!" He was influenced by others to do evil.

In the first chapter of Proverbs there is a classic example of being influenced or pulled into sin. We might say that it includes both the call of the Turkey and the Eagle. So pick your flock.

Birds of a Feather

TURKEY CALLS

With or without their heads on, domestic turkeys are not very bright. The same cannot be said about wild turkeys. They are incredibly intelligent animals with some of the most incredible natural defense mechanisms in existence. They have superb sight, hearing, and smell, and travel in flocks, which multiplies the effectiveness of all those senses. I know from personal experience that they are one of the most, if not **the** most, challenging North American animals to hunt. That is especially true when you hunt with a bow and arrow. Several of the best-known bowhunting writers in America say that harvesting a wild turkey with a bow is the greatest trophy a bowhunter could attempt. Been there—done that, and I agree completely.

There is another kind of turkey that we need to think about. They have two legs and they flock together, but even though they can be wild, they tend to be more like the domestic turkey—not very bright. Anyone who flocks after evil isn't very bright, or to use the biblical term, they're foolish.

No, we haven't changed birds. A turkey is not only a feathered friend, but in an idiomatic way we used the name to describe those whom we disapprove of or at least think of in a negative way. That aggressive driver we discussed earlier, who does stupid and dangerous things on the road? He's a turkey! That cop who thought he was Dirty Harry and treated people like peons? He's a turkey, too! Those folks who forgot all that God had done, who got impatient waiting for Moses to return and forced Aaron to build a Golden Calf? They were turkeys also! (Soon to be sliced turkeys. Sorry.)

Turkeys strut and call, trying to attract others to become part of their flock. Solomon gives us an example of what they might say.

> . . . *"Come with us,*
> *Let us lie in wait for blood,*
> *Let us ambush the innocent without cause;*
> *Let us swallow them alive like Sheol,*
> *Even whole, as those who go down to the pit;*
> *We will find all kinds of precious wealth,*
> *We will fill our houses with spoil;*
> *Throw in your lot with us,*
> *We shall all have one purse."*
>
> –Proverbs 1:11-14

Even in this graphic Hebrew poetry we recognize the pull of peer pressure. "Come with us," join us, be part of the team, and feel a sense of belonging and acceptance. In this instance, there seems to be an appeal to pride. These turkeys are professional criminals, an organized gang, and they are inviting the novice to be part of their group.[3] That's pretty heady stuff for a young guy seeking recognition and acceptance. It's an instant stroke to the ego and a very hard offer to turn down. Because the self-esteem is momentarily pumped up, it's difficult to see the big picture of what this will lead to. Right now it's merely a matter of being included, and he can't see down the road to the disastrous results of joining their flock.

How many movies and TV shows have had as a plot, or a subplot: The young person gets pulled into a gang or some scheme, only to discover that it turned into something far more terrible than they ever imagined? It reminds me of that great Broadway musical *Oliver*. The story of the little boy who escapes from the oppressive orphanage and ends up befriending a boy called The Artful Dodger. He takes Oliver to meet a large group of boys, all of whom have been trained to be pick-pockets by a dirty old man named Fagan. Fagan soon convinces the boy to join them as he sings the song "You've Got to Pick a Pocket or Two." Oliver, of course, soon realizes that this was a big mistake. Oliver lived "happily ever after," but not everyone who experiences the enticement to do evil has such an ending.

In Solomon's illustration, not only is there an enticement to belong, but there's the attraction of a plan. Most people don't have a plan for anything, but that's especially true of young people. They don't know enough or have enough experience to have any plan of action laid out for themselves. While they are especially susceptible to peer-pressure plans, people of all ages are pulled into following leaders who have it all worked out. Names like David Koresh, Jim Jones, Tim McVey, Adolf Hitler, and Charles Manson come to mind. These may all be twentieth century evil enticers, but people of similar ilk have been around since "men began to multiply on the face of the earth" (Genesis 6:1).

There was a time when this Proverb seemed too cruel and too graphic for me to see its relevance. "Come on," I thought, "who would be enticed to join a group of thugs who intend to commit cold-blooded murder?" Now, after years of hearing of just that kind of thing nearly every night on the *News*, it doesn't seem extreme in the least. In fact, the description of "lie in wait for blood" and "let us ambush the innocent without cause," sounds like something from our evening *News*. We've seen video recordings of store clerks being gunned down by robbers for no reason at all. We've been shocked to hear about employees and customers at fast-food restaurants or ice cream parlors being systematically executed by thieves who didn't want to leave any witnesses.

This plan is ruthless. The victims are "innocent" and totally undeserving of such vicious treatment. To "swallow them alive like Sheol" is a grossly poetic way of saying that the victims, who are full of life and a long way from the grave, will be completely removed from the living like a body is completely buried in a grave. They will be "like those under whose feet the earth is suddenly opened, so that, without leaving any trace behind, they sink into the grave. . . ."[4]

There is also a promise in the plan. "We will find all kinds of precious wealth, We will fill our house with spoil." Easy money! "Come with us" and you will have all your dreams fulfilled. "Come on, enjoy the good life!"

Can't you visualize the young boy looking at the drug dealer, who has new cloths, a flashy car, and a ring on every finger, and wishing he could have all that? We are hearing that used as an explanation or excuse for why so many, especially from the inner city, are pulled into crime. "They're trapped," goes the argument, "and the only way they see to better themselves and get the things in life they'd never otherwise get is to chose a life of crime." It seems to me that a lot of people have a twisted idea of what it means to "better themselves," and they certainly have some twisted priorities if getting "things" is done at the expense of ruined and destroyed lives.

It's nothing new! It has been going on since long before Solomon wrote about it. There have always been those who found "all kinds of wealth" and filled their "houses with spoil" at the cost of innocent lives. When Jesus used an illustration of a man who "fell among robbers, and they stripped him and beat him, and went off leaving him half dead," He was using something that was a common part of their culture (Luke 10:30). It may have been more dangerous for someone to walk the rural roads alone in Jesus' day than it is for us to do the same today on city streets at night.

The allure of easy money has caused criminals to go from being petty thieves to cold-blooded killers. It has made politicians and preachers commit fraud and destroy the lives of good, trusting people. They conclude that easy money brings easy living, which is an incredible lie in itself, but they don't see that it requires perverted thinking. A "church-going" man once commented to me that if he could get away with it, he'd be tempted, "for one time only," to smuggle a shipment of drugs into the country. His thinking was that just one shipment of drugs would make him a millionaire and he'd never have to do it again. The most important part of course, is that he'd "have it made" for the rest of his life. He never considered the thousands of lives hurt, with some being killed, as his "one time only" batch of drugs was marketed across the nation.

The promise in this plan not only includes wealth, but it includes acceptance. "Throw in your lot with us," say the turkeys, and "we shall all have one

I Knew That!

purse," which simply means you'll be accepted into the flock. We've mentioned this point before, but it deserves double attention. Most people crave acceptance, and will do amazing things to get it.

We have all paid a price to belong to a group. It may have been money, in the form of dues, or goods and services donated, or incredibly stupid things as part of an initiation. If you've ever been in the military, in sports, in clubs, or in a college fraternity or sorority you've done things to get accepted. Most of the time it's harmless, even fun things, but sometimes, when people have lost their values in life, the price is ungodly. We've all heard stories on the evening *News* about gangs requiring robberies, rapes, or murders as an entrance requirement. There's always someone who is willing to do the unthinkable just to share in the "one purse."

EAGLE SOARING

I have been blessed to see eagles soaring on several occasions and in several different states. I have also seen scores of them on wildlife programs, usually on the Discovery Channel. The picture that sticks out in my mind though isn't the distant eagle gliding around the Alaskan sky, or the pin-point accuracy of an eagle plucking a fish from the water while flying at an incredible speed. I remember eagles most from my early childhood visits to the National Zoo in Washington, D.C. Back then, in the Dark Ages of course, the eagle cage was the only cage that had a somewhat natural setting. The huge cage enclosed the side of a cliff and the eagles sat on perches way up in the top. When it was time to feed them, the zookeeper would turn live mice loose on the floor of the cage and the eagles would swoop down and scoop them up. It was amazing to watch.

Because of poor timing, we rarely got to see the feeding, but I still enjoyed just looking at them. All the other birds in all the other cages squawked and constantly fluttered around their cages, but not the eagle. He would sit majestically, watching, not missing a thing, and seemed to be aloof from all the other birds. The eagles seemed to soar even when they weren't flying.

While we probably do the animal kingdom a disservice by ascribing human characteristics and emotions to them, I am sure that the reason the eagle is our national symbol comes from its look of strength, confidence, and wisdom we see in them. On the other hand, if Benjamin Franklin had had his way, our national bird would be the turkey, and we'd probably think of the eagle as stuck-up and stupid, and the turkey as proud and majestic. But he didn't—and we don't—so my symbolism still counts!

There are more turkeys out there than eagles. That's true both literally and

Birds of a Feather

figuratively. If turkeys symbolize dumb advice, then eagles symbolize wise advice. We've heard from the turkeys already, in verses 11 through 14 of Proverbs 1, so let's make sure we hear from the eagles. Their advice is:

> My son, if sinners entice you,
> Do not consent.
>
> –v. 10

> My son, do not walk in the way with them.
> Keep your feet from their path,
> For their feet run to evil
> And they hasten to shed blood.
> Indeed, it is useless to spread the baited net
> In the sight of any bird;
> But they lie in wait for their own blood;
> They ambush their own lives.
> So are the ways of everyone who gains by violence;
> It takes away the life of its possessors.
>
> –vv. 15-19

The charge to "not consent" and "do not walk" is simply another way of saying don't listen to them or follow them. Sometimes we get caught up in things by default. We didn't say yes or no, we just followed along and became caught up in the flow of things. Most people believe that is how Lot ended up in the city of Sodom. Back in Genesis 13, Abraham gave Lot the first choice of where to live, and he chose to settle "in the cities of the valley, and moved his tents as far as Sodom. Now the men of Sodom were wicked exceedingly and sinners against the LORD" (vv. 12-13). The next time we read about Lot and his family, they're out of their tents and residents in the city, but obviously not like the people in the city (Genesis 19). How did that happen? It is implied that they are, at least to some degree, righteous people and if six more just like them had been found, God wouldn't have destroyed Sodom and Gomorrah. It seems like they just "followed the crowd" and found themselves in one of history's most sinful cities.

The wise person will not compromise and will not be influenced to follow a bunch of thugs. Stay out of their way! Don't even walk on the same street as they walk on! Avoid them like the plague! They are attracted to evil like hogs are to slop—they run to it and trample anything or anyone that gets in their way.

I Knew That!

The closing verses are a clear warning any way you want to interpret them. There are several different ways to interpret the sentence, "It is useless to spread the net in the eyes of any bird; but they lie in wait for their own blood; they ambush their own lives." The most logical interpretation seems to be that these "turkeys" are in such a hurry to steal and kill that they don't have the brains of the average bird. A bird can see that a net is being set and it will change course to keep from getting snagged by it, but not these greedy characters. They know that they are going to get caught, that they are preparing their own doom, but they do it anyway. Not very smart! "They ambush their own lives," by building the net that will catch them and staying on a course of action that will lead them right into it.

We must remember that there are spiritual laws that are absolute and irrefutable. Some natural laws can be overcome, postponed, or circumvented, but not so with spiritual laws. God doesn't miss anything Everything will be judged, whether it was done in secret or in the open. (Ecclesiastes 12:14; Hebrews 9:27). It's called the law of sowing and reaping. What ever we sow, we will reap. If we sow sin, we will reap corruption, but if we sow to the Spirit, we will reap eternal life (Galatians 6:7). Again, God doesn't miss anything. As Moses said to the tribes of Reuben and Gad about keeping their promise to help the other tribes conquer the promised land, "Be sure your sin will find you out" (Numbers 32:23).

Following a flock of turkeys to do evil is a no-win situation any way you want to look at it. As Solomon said, "So are the ways of everyone who gains by violence; it takes away the life of its possessors." I especially like the use of the word "everyone." No one ever really gets away with anything evil. If you choose to be with turkeys, you'll get plucked—sooner or later!

FINAL FEATHER FOCUS

Not too long ago my family went through a very difficult period. We were hurt deeply by some people we'd served and known for several years. It involved disappointment and betrayal on a level I had never experienced before. I expected better from Christians and people who claimed friendship with me, and it was a very disheartening and discouraging time.

Personally, and as a family, we grew during that experience. It was because we turned it over to God and humbly waited for Him to show us what He wanted done. Another reason I can look back on it as a positive experience is because of all the wonderful, loving, Christlike people God sent to help us get through it. There were people praying for us, sending us cards and letters, and just giving us loads of hugs and acts of encouragement. There were friends who prayed with me, counseled with me, cried with me, and studied God's Word with me. They gave advice, perspective, insights, hopes, and dreams. They built me up but allowed me to learn from being humbled. They pointed me to God's plans and not Satan's attacks. They showed me Christlike attitudes so I wouldn't think about the un-Christlike actions. They were "the wind beneath my wings" so that I could soar above it all. They showed me how important it is to pick your flock carefully.

If you want to soar like an eagle, you need to be with those who will help you soar! Choose to be part of God's flock because "those who wait for the LORD Will gain new strength; They will mount up with wings like eagles. . . ." (Isaiah 40:31). Quit saying, "I knew that" and start saying, "I'll do that!"

NOTES
1. Barclay, William, *The Letters to the Corinthians*, The Daily Study Bible Series (Philadelphia: Westminster, 1975), pp. 154-155.
2. "1 Corinthians," *The Expositor's Bible Commentary*, vol. 10 (Grand Rapids: Zondervan, 1991), p. 288.
3. "Proverbs," *The Expositor's Bible Commentary*, vol. 5, p. 908.
4. C.F. Keil and F. Delitzch, *Commentary On The Old Testament*, vol. VI (Grand Rapids: Eerdman's), Reprint 1980, p. 63.

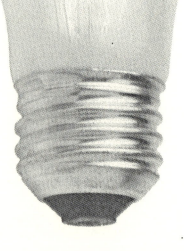

CHAPTER FOUR
"Getting Off Our High Horses"

The trip from Jerusalem had been rather uneventful. Long days in the saddle, riding under the hot sun, being lulled to sleepiness by the rhythmic sound of hooves hitting packed dirt and the counter-point of creaking leather. Saul and his detachment of temple guards had made good time, enjoyed the picturesque countryside, and been bolstered by the deferential treatment given to them by the common people and religious leaders in the cities and towns they passed through. After all, they were officials from the Jerusalem synagogue, and Saul was widely known as an "up-and-comer" in the Sandhedrin. He was one of the young firebrands who already had a reputation as a religious scholar and protector of orthodoxy. In fact, the purpose of this trip described in Acts chapter 9 was to clean out a nest of that new sect, call the Way, which had cropped up in Damascus. He'd already done a pretty good job of cleaning up Jerusalem. The ones who hadn't been killed or imprisoned had either gone underground or scattered to other towns like Damascus. Now, with letters in hand from the high priest in Jerusalem, he was on a mission to round up as many of those heretical Way followers as he could and bring them back for trial. In the name of The Law, he was a temple bounty hunter on a mission from Jehovah.

The daytime boredom was shattered by a blinding light that shot down from the sky. Like a bolt of lightening, it struck Saul and knocked him off his horse to the ground. The rest of the detachment were jolted into paralysis and became unwitting spectators to the beginning of their boss's transformation.

A voice spoke to him, as he sat up on the ground trying to rub the blinding dust from his eyes. "Saul, Saul, why are you persecuting Me?" it said. He froze. That was not the voice of one of his men. "Who are you," he muttered, and then added, "Lord?" He strained to see, but nothing came into focus. His heart was pounding with fear as he waited for a reply.

"I am Jesus whom you are persecuting," came the answer.

I Knew That!

His head dropped to his chest. His heart that only moments ago had been filled with pride, purpose, and persecution, now was broken and contrite. Pictures of people flashed across his mind. He remembered Steven looking to heaven as stones crashed against his body. Saul had his arms full of coats at the time, or he'd have been pitching rocks, too. He remembered men and women being dragged off to prison in chains, as family members pleaded for mercy and children cried in terror. He recalled the cheers of the temple crowd as he proclaimed what he was going to do with all those followers of the Carpenter yet to be caught. He felt the pats on the back from the high priest and other members of the Sandhedrin as reports flowed in about all the "disciples" who were fleeing for their lives to regions of Judea and Samaria.

His eyes filled with tears, but he still couldn't see anything. He suddenly realized that God was punishing him for not recognizing His Messiah, and he braced himself for the next bolt of lightening. Instead he heard Jesus say, ". . . get up and enter the city, and it will be told you what you must do."

The temple guards had to lead him by the hand all the way into Damascus, where for three days he fasted and prayed to God for forgiveness. God answered his prayers and fulfilled His own plans by sending Ananias to heal his sight and his soul. What an incredible relief it must have been to hear Ananias say, "And now why do you delay? Arise and be baptized, and wash away your sins, calling on His name" (Acts 22:16).

You know the ending—he lived holy ever after!

God had plans for Saul, who was soon to be called Paul, but before he could be used, he had to first get off his high horse and fall on his face before God.

I don't know where it came from, but my mother used to say it and I remember John Wayne saying it in at least one movie, so that makes it nearly sacred. I can hear the Duke's voice clearly saying, "Get down off your high horse, Mister!" The result was an instant case of meekness. My mother would usually say it about someone who was acting a little too cocky or arrogant. She never had to explain it to me; it just seemed to make perfect sense. Some folks feel superior to others. You know—"high and mighty." The only cure for this self-exaltation was a good thumping off that high horse they put themselves on.

I suspect it had its roots (and we Roots love to get to the root of things) in the days of old when the aristocracy had the huge, healthy horses, and they would ride around looking down on the lowly peons and peasants. Some people needed to be on a literal horse to look down on others, but some could do it no matter at what altitude their heads happened to be. Even today, the urge to want to be above others leads to wearing high heels, lifts, and/or cowboy boots. But again, to some it's a state of mind. To God it's pride and it's sin.

Getting Off Our High Horses

EQUINE EXTRICATION

We've all taken a turn on a "high horse" at one time or another in our lives. Those who were smart enough to observe and learn from others got down off that horse pretty quickly. Others of us had to get knocked out of the saddle several times before the lesson sunk in. Each time we picked ourselves up off the ground, we brushed the dirt off, smacked our foreheads, and said, "I knew that!" Some, the really hardheaded, climbed back up on that horse and chose to live there. To them the rarefied air at that altitude smells sweeter, but to God it's an altitude with an attitude that stinks.

Pride is not always bad. Like many things, it must be kept in balance—a particular context. In the Bible, the words "pride" and "proud" are always used in a bad sense. The Greek words used for pride mean "vainglory . . . haughty . . . puffed up . . . (or) high-minded."[1] Proud, in biblical Greek, "signifies showing oneself above others, pre-eminent; (and) is always used in Scripture in the bad sense of arrogant (or) disdainful."[2]

In contemporary usage, pride does have a good side when used in a positive, and even humble, context. One of the definitions for pride in our dictionary is "a sense of one's own dignity; self-respect." One can always have too much of that, but we generally encourage our children to have self-respect. Another way of defining pride is having "delight or satisfaction in one's achievements, children, etc.; a person or thing in which pride is taken." One of the definitions for being proud is to be "highly pleased with" some one or thing.[3]

We need to take pride in ourselves and care about cleanliness and modesty. Can we over-do it? Sure, but we've all seen what happens when people don't care enough to take proper care of themselves. It's natural to be proud of your children. I've watched my three participate in sports, plays, music competitions, programs, and concerts. They've received many awards and public recognition. Was I proud of them? Absolutely! So proud it brought tears to my eyes and prayers to my lips. There has been nothing that has been more humbling to me than to realize how God has blessed me with such wonderful children. When I hear them sing praises to God, whether it's in one of their special singing groups, the Harding University chorus, or just sitting around our living room—you can bet I'm proud. I'm proud that they love Jesus and are committed to living for Him.

We ought to be proud of our families! We ought to be proud of our church too! I'm talking about, oddly enough, a godly pride. A godly pride is thankful and humble, and gives all the glory to God. Godly pride ". . . does not brag and is not arrogant, does not act unbecomingly; it does not seek its own, is not provoked, does not take into account a wrong suffered, does not rejoice in unrighteousness, but rejoices in the truth; bears all things, believes all things, hopes all things, endures all things" (1 Corinthians 13:4-7). Godly pride is "highly pleased" with what makes God "highly pleased."

Was God "highly pleased" with Jesus at His baptism by John? (Matthew 3:16-17). Was He "highly pleased" with Jesus on the mount of transfiguration? (Matthew 17:5). If He was, and I think that is rather obvious, would it not be appropriate to say that He was proud of Jesus? In fact, Jesus told several parables about masters, owners, or such like, who were "highly pleased" with what their servant or laborer did. Godly pride is referred to, even if it is never specifically called that.

The reason I emphasize this is to make the simple point that pride can be healthy or unhealthy, good or bad, godly or ungodly. It depends on what it is for and about. Another good example of this is jealousy. Jealousy is usually thought of as ungodly, yet He said, "I am a jealous God" (Exodus 20:5; 34:14; Deuteronomy 4:24). Paul told the church at Corinth, "I am jealous for you with a godly jealousy" (2 Corinthians 11:2). There is no contradiction in this. There are things that we must be jealous about—godly things. God was jealous about Israel's unfaithfulness, as Paul was about the church in Corinth. This has nothing to do with being selfish, greedy, covetous, envious, and ungodly, which is the sinful kind of jealousy we usually think of first.

Unlike sinful pride and jealousy, we need godly pride and godly jealousy. Ungodly pride is haughty, egotistical, conceited, self-centered, self-absorbed, and self-condemning. This kind of pride is really the result of an out-of-balance self-esteem. We need to feel good about ourselves, but not *too* good. The elements of self-esteem are security, significance, and competence. We all need a healthy dose of each of these elements in order not to feel insecure, insignificant, or incompetent, but too much of these, and we go from "I'm secure" to "I'm in charge," from "I count" to "I'm the most important," and from "I can" to "I'm the best." The tendency to over-inflate the ego is just as dangerous as having a deflated ego.

Amazingly enough, a haughty pride can come from either end of the imbalance if it is taken to the extreme. Sometimes people become very prideful to compensate for their poor self-esteem. The schoolyard bully and the strutting gang member may really be manufacturing their self-importance to cover up their lack of self-worth. After all, what is there to be proud of when you are talking about crime, hate, and ignorance?

At the other end of the out-of-balance self-esteem are those who truly think they are more important, better, or superior to others. They just have an exalted view of themselves. It may be because of economics, education, power, prejudice, or any number of things, but it's a haughty spirit and it's sinful in God's eyes.

Getting Off Our High Horses

This kind of pride, the haughty self-centered pride, is dangerous. Not only is it dangerous to all those who get stepped on, abused, enslaved, ridiculed, snubbed, persecuted, and exterminated by such people, but it's dangerous to the prideful person, too. The danger to them comes from the fact that God doesn't coexist with pride. Pride is replacing God with self. Maybe that's why the Bible says, "For God is opposed to the proud, but gives grace to the humble" (1 Peter 5:5).

Talk about a dangerous position to be in! God is opposed or against those who are proud! What does it mean to have God against you? It's a no-win situation! As you go charging across the field of battle on your loyal steed, feeling free and invulnerable, you will eventually begin to see your opposition clearly. Before it's too late, recognize that your opposition is God, get down of your high horse, and surrender immediately.

One of the most sobering questions we all must think about is if God is opposed to us, because of our pride, what might He do to humble us? We have plenty of examples of God bringing people, cities, and even nations to their knees. What might He decide to use for us? A thorn in the flesh, like He did with Paul? A death in the family, like He did with David? How about the threat of annihilation, like He did with Nineveh? He may not be the cause, but what might He allow to happen to us in order to develop a humble spirit in us? A financial crash, a serious health problem, a job loss, or some form of rejection or disappointment? These things cause some to blame God, while others learn to humbly depend on Him.

Here's another thought-provoking question. If we are saved by grace (Ephesians 2:8), and God gives grace to the humble (James 4:6), does that mean that the proud are lost? Let's see? God is opposed to them, they are guilty of idolatry because they replace God with self, and they cannot receive grace. That sounds like three strikes to me! Of course it's not up to us to do the judging because we are all sinners saved by the grace of God. But, that's the point—there is no grace for the prideful. I've heard hundreds, maybe thousands of sermons on what's essential for salvation, but I've never heard anyone mention humility. Is humility essential to salvation? God gives grace to the humble! Humility is optional for salvation only if grace is optional, and we all know that's not an option.

Actually, this gets us back to where we started. Grace is the only answer to the balance problem. How can we have a healthy pride that doesn't turn into an ungodly pride, and how can we have humility without letting it turn into poor self-esteem? It's impossible for us to have such a balance separate and apart from grace. Our sense of worth must come from God. He declares us important, lovable, and worth saving. He made us, offered His Son for us, adopted us, and prepared heaven for us. That means we are incredibly important! We are children of God, brothers and sisters of Jesus, royal priests, and heaven-bound saints! We are saved by His grace!

But, we must emphasize, it is *His* grace not ours! We are unbelievably important, but at the same time, we don't deserve it. Grace is undeserved favor, and we were and are immensely undeserving. While we are buoyed by love we are humbled by sacrifice. We are important, but at the same time we are nothing; we are special, but we are also sinners, and we are redeemed, but at a tremendous cost. We are proud to be children of God and humbled by our unworthiness. Only grace can give balance to the impossible. Only grace can put courage into humility while at the same time kicking selfishness out of pride.

HORSE TRADING

David was "knocked off his high horse" by Nathan the prophet, who told him a story that had both a punch and a punch line. You may remember that David had arrogantly committed adultery with Bathsheba and then arranged for her husband Uriah to be killed in battle so that he could marry her. The Bible says, "But the thing that David had done was evil in the sight of the LORD" (2 Samuel 11:27).

God sent Nathan to tell David a story. The story was about a poor man who had only one little lamb and it was taken by a rich man, who had many flocks of his own. David was incensed by the story and swore that the selfish, insensitive rich man would pay "fourfold" restitution for doing such a terrible thing. Nathan said to him, "You are the man!" Though not recorded in Scripture, there was a huge smacking sound as David's humbled spirit descended from his lofty perch to the royal floor (2 Samuel 12:1-15).

Years later David wrote a song about this experience. In it he tells about his praying to God for a "clean heart . . . a steadfast spirit" and the restoration in him of "the joy of Your salvation." He goes on to sing, "For You do not delight in sacrifice, otherwise I would give it; You are not pleased with burnt offering. The sacrifices of God are a broken spirit; A broken and a contrite heart, O God, You will not despise" (Psalm 51).

David learned that pride was a "high horse" that was much too dangerous to ride, and certainly too expensive to own. He traded it in for a broken and contrite heart. His son Solomon, with all his wisdom, didn't learn that lesson from his dad, but from his own experiences being thrown from that same mustang. Here are some of the things he learned.

Getting Off Our High Horses

When pride comes, then comes dishonor,
But with the humble is wisdom.
—Proverbs 11:2

Isn't it ironic that we tend to associate pride with honor, but the Holy Spirit associates pride with dishonor? What's honorable about the absence of humility? To elevate self is to devalue God, and that's not only a dishonor to Him but to one's self. Satan loves to make us believe that we look good all puffed up with ourselves. Pride masquerades as confidence, in control, in charge, leadership ability, and toughness. All it is in reality is self-serving, ego inflating, and haughty. It dishonors honesty, compassion, humility, and godliness. The world may say, "you've got your act together," but God just says it's an act.

The word dishonor is translated "disgrace" in the NIV Bible. While they are synonyms, disgrace has a stronger negative connotation to me. In my experience, the charge of dishonoring something or someone seems like a mild reprimand, but being a disgrace is a strong indictment. Maybe I get that from the movies, but hearing someone say, "You have dishonored your badge," just doesn't hit as hard as "You are a disgrace to your badge!"

There's an interesting parallel to what we pointed out earlier. The prefix "dis" is used to mean "not." That means that disgrace is not-grace, the absence of grace, or the opposite of grace. That shouldn't come as a surprise because remember to whom God gives grace? The humble! He opposes the proud (James 4:6).

How many dishonorable or disgraceful things have been done because of pride? In the name of national pride, Hitler went to war against most of the world. Religious pride has caused wars, crusades, terrorism, "ethnic cleansing," and genocide. Racial pride has led to lynchings, assassinations, fire bombings, riots, and hate groups. The list of things that have resulted from political pride runs the gamut from "dirty tricks" to bombed government building and abortion clinic. The people who've done all these things are quite proud of themselves. God says, "When pride comes, then comes dishonor."

How many stupid things have been done because someone's pride was challenged? When I was in high school, a Christian boarding school, we had strict rules about girls being around the boy's dorm and vice versa. Actually, the rule was simple; STAY AWAY! One day two girls forgot or ignored that rule and cut through the front yard of the boy's dorm. Two boys saw them coming and dared each other to teach the girls a lesson. Alone, neither one of those guys would have done what they did, but they challenged each others' pride and there was no turning back. They proceeded to stick their naked backsides out second floor windows and provide a planetary symbol for the ladies to think about.

It's easy, even today, to giggle about that juvenile act, but it was an incredibly dumb thing to do at a Christian school. The administration saw nothing funny about it and expelled both of them. (The two boys not the girls.) A similar incident happened at a high school graduation a couple of years ago. A graduating male flashed the audience after he was handed his diploma. It was on the national news because he was arrested for indecent exposure. When he was asked why he did it he simply explained that some friends dared him to do it. Unfortunately, they weren't the ones who were sentenced to two days in jail and one hundred hours of community service. They also weren't the ones who were dishonored.

We need to hear Solomon's warning not just contemplate his proverbial saying. He is pointing out a fact of life, and more importantly, a biblical truth. The proud will be brought down. They will have their ego deflated. When pride comes, one may feel important on that wild high horse, but the proud is merely marking time until the fall. Hopefully one can learn through education, experiences, and observation, and dismount before God does the job for them. As Solomon said, ". . . with the humble is wisdom." It's only when we get off that high horse that we really start learning and growing.

BRONCO BREEDING

In the hazy gray of a Texas pre-dawn I was still getting settled into my tree stand for a morning of deer hunting. I caught movement out of the corner of my eye and I turned to see a large-bodied animal moving like a ghost on the game trail just twenty yards away. The body was big enough to be a deer, but even in the gray light I could tell that the legs were much too short. It only took another second to identify the largest bobcat I have ever seen. I only got to watch him for a few moments because as I reached for my bow, which was hanging on a tree hook, the wild cat spotted me. For a second I thought he was going to come after me. He crouched down and started stalking towards me. I was completely camouflaged from head to toe, but he still had me pegged in seconds as a threat, and shot out of there like a missile.

What I remember most about that experience was the size of that bobcat and the replaying of an old sermon illustration that went through my mind as I watched him. A little boy asked his dad, "Why are wildcats wild?" The dad thought a second and answered, "Because their moms and dads are wild." Simple but true.

Just as wildcats breed wildcats, pride breeds pride or even something worse. Solomon said,

Getting Off Our High Horses

*Pride only breeds quarrels,
but wisdom is found in those who
take advice.*
—Proverbs 13:10 NIV

I wonder if there is such a thing as a quarrel that doesn't have its roots in pride? I'm sure there is an exception somewhere, but it is the exception not the rule. Prideful people don't listen to others. Why should they, they have all the answers. Their eyes may be looking at you, but their brains aren't seeking understanding they're merely formulating the defense. You can't have an open and honest discussion with a prideful know-it-all. The best you can hope for is an argument, and that's not much of a choice.

Even if you do not lead a prideful lifestyle, you probably have some areas of knowledge in which you are very experienced and see yourself as some form of an expert. Isn't it difficult to not be prideful about your expertise when the discussion finally gets to "your area?" Isn't it hard to keep from saying things like, "Excuse me, but I am an expert in this field so just be quiet and listen to what I can give you!" Maybe you've said, "Well I don't know a lot about a lot of things, but I do know about this!" Or maybe you've used this prideful phrase, "I've spent most of my life studying this and I know what I'm talking about!"

When you see yourself as an expert, you're ready to fight and defend your preeminence in that area. Hear it again—pride only breeds quarrels. Unless you are a couple of cartoon chipmunks, you never argue over humility.

Such is the sad irony of so-called "religious discussions." Has there ever really been an honest and open religious debate where anyone listened with the intent of learning anything new from his or her opponent? There is a lot of pride in being spiritually correct. The oft heard comment, "Open your Bible and show us where we are doing anything wrong and we will change," is more often a haughty statement of pride in the belief that we couldn't possibly be doing anything wrong. So we don't study, we arm ourselves; we don't share, we refute; and we don't learn, we just reinforce orthodoxy.

Wouldn't it be interesting to have a transcript of what was said when the apostles had that argument about whom of their group was the greatest? The Bible says it was "an argument" (Luke 9:46). People don't argue over humility! No one argues about being unselfish, or being a servant, or being Christlike. These guys were arguing about who was the greatest because they all were quite proud of being the "chosen few." The Bible says that Jesus knew what they were thinking in their hearts. He could see the pride behind their quarrel, so He decided it was time for a dramatic visual illustration.

I Knew That!

As these future pillars of faith argued about who was more important to Jesus, He pulled a small child to His side and essentially told them, "He's my main man!" I suspect that the sight of twelve grown men dropping their jaws was memorable. Jesus told them that they needed to treat that child as if he were Jesus Himself. Then He added, "and whoever receives Me receives Him who sent Me." What a chain of importance! The child was connected to Jesus and thus to God the Father. He, that child, was whom God considered great!

They must have started shuffling their feet and lowering their heads about that time as they grasped the lesson of childlike humility. God wants humble hearts not prideful power brokers! Then, to really hammer the point home, Jesus declared, "for he who is least among you, this is the one who is great." Ouch! I wonder if they ever argued about who was the least?

What a hard lesson to learn! Right after Jesus taught them that powerful lesson, John pointed out that others besides the apostles were casting out demons in His name, and they had tried to stop them. Apparently, because of the context, John wasn't worried about defending Jesus as much as he was concerned about losing their position as "The Apostles" of Jesus. Jesus told him not to stop them "for he who is not against you is for you." He was saying look through the eyes of humility not pride. See the good they do and not the prestige you think you're losing.

Not too long after that exchange, John and his brother James became irate when a Samaritan town rejected Jesus. Their response was not sadness or concern for those souls, but "Lord, do you want us to command fire to come down from heaven and consume them?" They made a big mistake! They not only were guided by pride, but also they assumed that Jesus felt the same way they did. "But He turned and rebuked them," the Bible says. Again, ouch! He turned and confronted them face-to-face! Why? They really didn't understand Him at all. In time they would, but at that point they were suffering from foot-in-mouth pride (Luke 9:46-55).

Pride breeds quarrels like garbage breeds flies. It's just a natural part of it. It makes the three-year-old child scream, "I can do it myself," and the thirteen-year-old girl disagree with everything you say. It makes the male ego focus more on control than common sense and compassion, and it makes the female instinct think "I can be just as stupid as any man." Pride makes us competitive, compulsive, and uncooperative. It fertilizes smugness, self-righteousness, and being opinionated. It makes us argumentative, unbending, and unforgiving. Unfortunately, it also makes us hateful, ungodly, and un-Christlike.

I have several shelves in my personal library filled with books about marriage, relationship building, and intimacy. I have preached, taught, and written

Getting Off Our High Horses

about marriage on more occasions than I could ever remember. I know what the surveys and statistics about marriage report in terms of the biggest problems in marriage. Nevertheless, while it may be statistically impossible to prove, I believe with all my heart that the biggest problem in any and all marriages—the cause of more arguments—the reason for more divorces—is pride. Long before there were any marriage counselors, books, and seminars on marriage, the Holy Spirit declared, "Pride only breeds quarrels." While not all quarrels come from pride, only a few don't. When what's needed is communication, but all you do is quarrel, it's pride on someone's part. It may be easier to say the problem is finances, sexual intimacy, or some unacceptable behavior, but the lack of communication behind the problem has its roots in pride.

Pride keeps people from talking, from giving, and from apologizing. Pride looks for excuses, finds fault, and fails to change. Pride is the cancer of marriage. It's curable, but it can be terminal.

Pride makes married people lay awake at night, inches away from their spouse, needing disparately to resolve conflict and share intimacy, but thinking "Let him (or her) make the first move." For years I have proclaimed to people, "If you don't communicate you speculate." Pride tells you to settle for speculation.

"Wisdom is found in those who take advice." The only person who won't take advice is the one who is too proud to take it. Pharaoh could have saved his people a great deal of hardship and grief if he'd only listened to Moses. He could have stopped the crisis at any point during the ten plagues, but NO! He was the top dog and no one was going to dictate to him what he should do—even if He called Himself Jehovah, the true and living God!

What a contrast there is between Pharaoh and Moses! Pharaoh's leadership style was based on power and pride, while Moses seemed to lead by example and humility. Ironically enough, he was the one with the real power because he was representing God. He didn't ever feel worthy for the task. In fact, he felt very inadequate, but God supplied his every need. Even after the incredible escape from Pharaoh and his army, which included the whole Red Sea experience, and being the sole autocratic leader of Israel, he still listened and accepted the advice of his father-in-law Jethro to delegate his judging responsibilities (Exodus 18). Even after being God's spokesman and hearing God give the Law, he was still described, "very humble, more than any man who was on the face of the earth" (Numbers 12:3).

Pride fosters stupidity. There is so much to learn and so many people from whom to learn, why would we ever want to limit ourselves because of pride? I need to learn from my children, and not feel like I have to be the know-it-all-dad! I need to listen to my wife, who has a far better perspective on sensitivity and compassion than I ever will! I need to study with my brothers, who may sit every week to hear my insights, but who collectively overshadow my knowledge like a library over a magazine! I need to seek the advice of scholars, older folks, simple people, professors, authors, farmers, street people, and folks with different cultures, ethnic backgrounds, and races. They don't care that I'm educated, published, affluent, listened to, and scheduled in advance! They need to know that I'm smart enough to learn from them! In return, the only thing I have that is worth sharing was given to me by the grace of God to be given away to others, and that is the Good News of Jesus Christ. Anything else about me is unimportant.

Real wisdom is found in those who listen and accept advice.

STALL BUSTING

Before I moved to begin a new ministry with a church in Texas, about ten years ago, one of the members of the official Minister Search Committee that picked me as a finalist told me about challenging the elders with a question. He in essence asked them, "Now what are you going to do if we hire a new minister and he's a wild buck who starts kicking the stall walls down? Are you going to be able to support him?" They assured him, that they wanted someone to come in and "shake things up" so that the church could get on with growing again. That turned out to be a less than honest reply, but I love the picture of a young, wild bronco kicking out the stall walls because it refused to be held back or penned up. Sometimes things need to be kicked over and destroyed, but not out of pride.

Proverbs has a plethora of passages portraying the pernicious propensity of pride to pull things to pieces. In other words, pride is destructive. As we close out this last section I want to look at some of the dramatic warnings in Proverbs that point out the perils of pride.

> *The LORD will tear down the house of the proud,*
> *But He will establish the boundary of the widow*
> *—Proverbs 15:25*

I spent seven years of my life in Arkansas and eight years in Texas, yet my closest encounter with a tornado was in Northern Virginia, just outside of Washington, D.C. At the time, I was riding with a police officer doing my police chaplain ministry, and the wind nearly blew the cruiser off the highway. Within seconds the police radio was crackling with calls about power outages, downed trees, and security alarms going off. As we drove past a

Getting Off Our High Horses

housing development where the houses were huge and expensive, we came on a most unusual sight. One of the two-story semi-mansions was missing its entire roof. The tornado had dropped down and hit that house without touching the houses on either side, which were only a few feet away. It took the whole roof, attic included, and set it down in the front yard of a Catholic Church across the street, about one hundred yards away.

It was so surreal to see nothing else damaged, except a plush house with the top missing. The road we were on behind the house was uphill from the house, so we could clearly see all the furniture and decorations in the now uncovered second floor. They were untouched and in place. Then, to make it look even stranger, the sun came out and spread a golden glow over the whole scene.

As it turned out, the homeowners were gone on vacation. I couldn't help but wonder how many times they stood in front of their house, swollen with pride, as they considered its size and beauty. It had been a gorgeous house, now it looked wrecked. The plastic cover that the Fire Department spread over the open roof didn't make it look any better. I knew they'd be crushed when they came home and saw what had happened to their pride and joy.

My house isn't big, but I like it! I've stood out front and looked it over and thought, "Nice looking house!" Most of the time, but not always, I remembered to say, "Thank you Lord."

The message of Solomon's proverb is obviously a warning to those who selfishly ignore the plight of the less fortunate. If you build yourself a castle and refuse to help those in need, get ready for a day of retribution! It may not be a house that you lose but something far more important!

On top of that lesson, I again hear the voice of the Holy Spirit shouting, "God opposes the proud, but He gives grace to the humble." In this proverb we hear about God tearing down a proud man's house, and I can't help but ask myself, what might God do to you and me to bring us to our knees—to humble us? We need to be careful about what we take pride in!

*Everyone who is proud in heart is an abomination to the LORD;
Assuredly, he will not be unpunished.*
–Proverbs 16:5

We are so "me" oriented that we don't spent much time thinking about how God feels about things. When God looks into our hearts and sees pride, the selfish haughty ungodly pride, He reacts violently. It deeply affects Him! He detests or hates what He sees!

Abomination probably doesn't carry the right connotation for us because it sounds too proper—too snowmanish! We all know what it means to detest something. What do you detest? What stirs your righteous emotions so much that you would judge it detestable, deplorable, and despicable? What kind of person could cause you to have such passionate negative feelings about him or her? How about a child molester? A rapist? A terrorist, who kills innocent women and children to achieve a political purpose? What about a politician who lies, cheats, and deceives a nation? How about a Hitler, a Stalin, or one of the contemporary leaders who inspire genocide, ethnic cleansing, and hatred of minorities, like we've seen in Bosnia, Serbia, and Iraq?

We might feel that pimps, pushers, and perverts are detestable, but to God the one "who is proud in heart" is detestable. That could be us! The proud of heart are the arrogant, the egotistical, and the presumptuous. We need to avoid the temptation to see this in terms of the "Big" crooks, the "Big" villains, and the "Big" sins. Being proud of heart is not just a matter of notoriety, enormity, or perversity. It's thinking you don't need God! When does feeling good become pride? When God is left out! When I listen to people tell me how wonderful my sermons are, how helpful my books have been, and what an incredible family I have, and I think, "Well, I really am pretty terrific!"—I've got a proud heart! Humility and thankfulness are the only response acceptable! God did it all and when I forget Him—when I replace Him in my heart with me—I run the risk of God detesting what He sees there.

I don't know how much of that He will put up with! He is always willing to forgive a penitent heart; but then a penitent heart is a changed heart. The unchanged heart "assuredly" will be punished. "Assuredly" means absolutely sure. The word in the original language literally means "hand to hand" as in shaking hands "to signify that something is guaranteed" or confirmed.[4] God's not going to miss or overlook a prideful heart. Pride is destructive and the most destructive part of pride is the way it destroys our relationship with our Father.

Pride goes before destruction,
And a haughty spirit before stumbling.
—Proverbs 16:18
Before destruction the heart of man is haughty,
But humility goes before honor.
—Proverbs 18:12

The prideful person can never stay that way. Pride is as temporary as bug stains on a car windshield before it rains. The sad part is that it can do an incredible amount of damage in its lifetime. It kills friendships, marriages, congrega-

Getting Off Our High Horses

tions, nations, teams, and souls. It doesn't build up—it tears down. It doesn't make a man a man—it makes a man a fool. It doesn't open hearts, minds, opportunities, futures, or relationships—it's in the closing business—it destroys those things. It's not enlightening, educational, or encouraging—it's just the opposite. It's not glue—it's a wedge. It's not a strong self-esteem—it's a shallow self-esteem. It's not good—it's ungodly. Pride is nothing to be proud of. As the Apostle John pointed out, ". . . the boastful pride of life, is not from the Father, but is from the world. The world is passing away. . . ." (1 John 2:16-17).

We cannot be used as instruments of God if we are full of pride. As Christians, it is only when we are humble that God can truly use us. Paul learned this through his struggle with his thorn in the flesh. We don't know what that thorn was, but the purpose, as Paul said, was "to keep me from exalting myself!" God told him, "My grace is sufficient for you, for power is perfected in weakness." His response to that insight from God was,

> *Most gladly, therefore, I will rather boast about my weaknesses, so that the power of Christ may dwell in me. Therefore I am well content with weaknesses, with insults, with distresses, with persecutions, with difficulties, for Christ's sake; for when I am weak, then I am strong.*
> –2 Corinthians 12:7-10

If we must be weak, which means to depend humbly on God before He can use us, it is obvious why pride can't be part of the equation. Have you ever heard such an amazingly unworldly concept as "for when I am weak, then I am strong?" It is only with and in God that it makes sense. It releases the power of Christ within us, which in turn gives us the strength to deal with anything the world can throw at us. It's a power that brings peace, contentment, and purpose to life.

If you don't have that, it may be because pride is blocking the way. Don't just slap your forehead and say, "I knew that." Listen to the Duke say, "Get off your high horse mister," and hear the King say, "Well done, good and faithful slave."

NOTES
1. Vine, W.E., *Vine's Expository Dictionary of New Testament Words*, vol. III (Old Tappan, NJ: Fleming H. Revell, 1966 edition), p. 210.
2. Ibid., p. 226.
3. *Webster's New World Dictionary of the American Language*, 1966, pp. 590, 598.
4. "Proverbs," *The Expositor's Bible Commentary*, vol. 5), p. 1003.

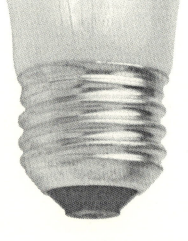
. . . those who wait for the LORD will gain new strength

CHAPTER FIVE
"Think Before You Speak"

One doesn't have to be the proverbial rocket scientist to take one look at the title of this chapter and recognize a major "I knew that" category. We have all said things we regretted saying. Sometimes it's when we reflect back over a period of time that we wish we hadn't said certain things, while other times we have regretted our words at the very moment they spewed forth from our lips. The regret can be for any number of reasons. We may have said something that was dumb, obviously ridiculous, and/or embarrassing. It showed our ignorance, our lack of experience, or maybe just how out-of-touch we were.

I was thirty years old, and seven years out of college when I went back to school to get my first graduate degree. I was really excited to be accepted to George Mason University's Master of History program. George Mason University is a very good school with an excellent history department, and it's smack-dab in the middle of some of America's richest history—northern Virginia. My love of history has always been primarily military history, so I was in heaven to have as my first two classes The French Revolution and The Civil War (though it was really just over a small part of it). The Civil War class was taught by the head of the Graduate History Department, who was nationally known as an expert in certain areas of the war. Needless to say, I was excited, but also intimidated by him and the class. To top it off, I was one of the youngest students in that class. Most of the other students were experienced high school history teachers who were getting their Master's degrees.

The class was great. We even had an incredible field trip to one of the major battlefields of the war, and the professor walked us all around it pointing out details and correcting the Historical Markers on the battlefield. One day in class he asked for suggestions for an undergraduate history reading list. He wanted some new ideas for books that would interest college students and help them enjoy their required history courses more. Since I was feeling relaxed and accepted, in the midst of several suggestions I offered up a book I'd recently read that was historical fiction. In other words, the main character was fictitious, but all the other characters and events where based on real historical facts. I thought it was educational yet enjoyable to read since it was a novel. Just the perfect thing for college kids who are bored out of their mind with cold history books.

I don't remember his exact words, but the professor quickly dismissed my suggestion as ridiculous and unworthy of such scholarly endeavors as he was talking about. I was totally embarrassed and felt like I'd been humiliated in the presence of my peers. It was the kind of thing that one would expect to happen in elementary school by a thoughtless teacher, but not among adults in a graduate class. I was so angry that I had very un-Christlike thoughts of violence. Then when I calmed down a little I thought about asking him some theological question and making him look dumb. Finally, I was able to reflect on the experience and realize that, considering the environment of smug academia, I had made a pretty dumb suggestion. I knew that! However, since I was a police chaplain at the time, for many days following that I had visions of how the cop I was riding with could stop that professor for some traffic offense. It's hard to recover from saying dumb things, and back then I was still working on grace.

It's one thing to be embarrassed because we say something ridiculous, and it's another to not accept the fact that it was the wrong thing to say. Have you ever been wrong about something and then been pig-headed about refusing to accept being mistaken? I sure have. Usually it's a discussion about sports, politics, or history, and I just know I'm right, so I hold my ground in spite of the opposition. The embarrassment over discovering I'm wrong is usually in direct proportion to the level of pig-headedness with which I refuse to budge.

Things like that hurt, cut, belittle, offend, degrade, and embarrass. All the more reason we should make sure the brain is running before we put the mouth in gear. We need to think before we speak. The worse kind of thoughtlessness may not be in forgetting to do something meaningful for someone, but in forgetting to think through what we are about to say.

How many times have you wished you could take back something you said? Words become guided missiles of destruction that cannot be called back once fired, whether in malice or thoughtlessness. I've launched plenty in my life. So many that I probably have developed a convenient mental block so I won't remember all those acts of terrorism. Speaking without thinking can make casualties out of both the senders and the receivers. Like the fallen Humpty Dumpty, it may be impossible to put all the pieces together again.

Think Before You Speak

Chances are pretty good that you are, or have been, a member of that missile launching army. You are in good company. History is full of people who wish they could retract things they said. There is no telling how many folks called Robert Fulton's idea for a steamboat "Fulton's Folly." Daniel Webster, in many public speeches, declared that a railroad system in America would never work. He said when frost got on the rails it would keep a train from moving. The *Chicago Times* in 1865 criticized Lincoln's "Gettysburg Address" as "silly, flat, and dish-watery utterances." In her 1933 book, Dorothy Thompson said that it only took her 50 seconds to determine that Adolf Hitler was a "formless, almost faceless man" and he'd "never become the dictator of Germany." And then there was Benjamin Franklin's prospective mother-in-law who was very hesitant to let her daughter marry a man who was about to open the United States' third printing shop. She thought that two shops were all the nation would ever need.

One of my favorite examples of speaking without thinking involves a sheet of paper that was found in the English War Office just after World War I. Back in 1911, a Nottingham plumber had submitted a design for what would later be called a tank. Across the top of the paper some office worker had written in red, "The man's mad."[1] What a difference a few years and a few million deaths can make!

I am confident that John, the apostle of love, spent a lot of years wishing he'd never suggested to Jesus that fire be called down from heaven to destroy the unreceptive town. And I'm equally sure that Peter rued the day he declared to Jesus that he would never deny Him. There's no doubt that he regretted the three statements of denial that caused him to weep bitterly.

James tells us, "But everyone must be quick to hear, slow to speak and slow to anger. . . ." (James 1:19). For some reason, most of us are quick to speak and slow to hear, and as a result, someone usually gets angry! Our parents told us over and over to think before we speak, but they didn't seem to heed their own advice. Then our schoolteachers kept pointing out to us that God gave us *two* ears and only *one* mouth, so we are expected to listen twice as much as we speak. Of course, that was back in the day when teachers could say the word "God" and, like teachers everywhere, they believed they were exempt from their own anatomical truism.

We like to be heard. We like to hear ourselves! We always believe that what we have to say is more important than what anyone else has to say. They should listen to us—not the other way around. It's all right for us to be thinking about what we are going to say next while they are talking; but they wouldn't dare do that when it's our turn to talk. The problem is that everyone is thinking the same way we are in terms of who needs to be heard and who needs to be doing the listening. It's amazing that there is ever any substantive communication!

Isn't it wonderful that the One person, who had the really important message and the complete right to be speaking, was also *The* consummate listener? The New Testament has the Words of Jesus, but it also describes His spirit. It never gave me a mental picture of a fast-talking, red-faced fanatic who demanded attention. I have always had a mental image of a relaxed, calm, and peaceful Jesus who quietly let the self-righteous Pharisees do all the yelling and talking while He listened and waited for them to seek His opinion.

There were times when He was forceful and outspoken, like when He cleansed the temple or denounced the hypocritical religious leaders, but He was never uptight and verbose. His comments were never out-of-line or questionable. He was very loving, thoughtful, and caring with everything He said. His comments and questions were very deliberate and thought out. He was a purpose-driven Lord whose only desire was to bring people closer to His Father. If we are going to be like Him, we must think before we speak.

This is a problem as old as time, so it shouldn't be any surprise to discover that Proverbs had much to say about the how, when, and why of speaking. There seems to be three key ideas that present themselves in Proverbs. Our speech needs to be thoughtful, appropriate, and controlled.

THOUGHTFUL

You are standing before a mob and they have blood in their eyes. They shove a woman to the ground just in front of you. That's when you notice that everyone is carrying stones. They have worked themselves into a frenzy and they are out for blood. This woman, they explain, has been caught participating in illicit sex. What she has done is an abomination and *the Law* says she should be stoned to death! They want to know what you think!

Wow! What a predicament! If I had been confronted with this scenario when I first came out of college and started preaching, I'd have said, "Hand me a stone!" Then, after several years of discovering what it means to be free in Christ and how wonderful His grace is, I'd have said, "You bunch of self-righteous hypocrites! What makes you think that your sins smell like Chanel Number 5 and hers stink?"

The longer I walk with Jesus, the more I appreciate His thoughtfulness. He didn't promote or condemn, He thought about it. As He knelt down and wrote in the sand, He mulled over the options and the needs, and gave the crowd a chance to do some thinking too. When He finally stood back up and challenged anyone without sin to throw the first stone, the crowd soon dispersed, from the oldest to the youngest. Sometimes the younger you are the harder it is to be thoughtful (John 8:1-11).

There are so many things that we can learn from that incredible story of Jesus and the adulterous woman. One of those lessons should be the importance of thoughtfulness. I believe Jesus wanted us to learn that lesson from this well-known story. His kneeling down and writing in the sand was for our benefit. He is God! (As in omniscient or all-knowing!) He didn't need time to think and be thoughtful! We do, so He showed us how to do it!

While thoughtfulness can be a simple act of logic or common sense, its greatest impact is when it is an act of unselfishness. Thoughtfulness usually implies thinking of others, what they need, and what I can do to assist them. Jesus was a thoughtful person because He was an unselfish person. If we are going to be like Him, we must become thoughtful. That means that we not only take the time to think, but we also think of others and not ourselves.

Thoughtfulness is an obvious quality of maturity. It takes time and maturity not to be rash in our deliberations and not to always think of ourselves. Solomon said,

> *The heart of the wise instructs his mouth*
> *And adds persuasiveness to his lips.*
> —Proverbs 16:23

If we would take the time to listen to what our heart says we could save a lot of wear-and-tear from that foot-in-mouth problem we all seem to have. Of course, if the heart is corrupt, what it teaches the mouth will be corrupt. This is the lesson that Jesus tried to get the Pharisees to understand, but they were more concerned with their traditions about cleanliness. Jesus said that it wasn't "what enters into the mouth" that makes a person unclean, "but what proceeds out of the mouth." The reason for this, He explained, is because "the things that proceed out of the mouth come from the heart, and those defile the man. For out of the heart come evil thoughts, murders, adulteries, fornications, thefts, false witness, slanders" (Matthew 15:18-19).

I would have been a lot more comfortable with Jesus' statements if He hadn't started His list with "evil thoughts." I don't think He was rating sins, but the fact that it's even on the list means that evil thinking is a symptom of heart trouble. We may not be murderers and adulterers, but we all struggle with what crosses our minds. If our speech betrays having evil thoughts we have heart trouble. When we have spiritual heart trouble we tend to be thoughtless rather than thoughtful. The problem with that is, as we've already seen, Jesus was thoughtful. If we aren't thoughtful, we aren't like Jesus!

Why is it so obvious when someone is speaking with wisdom? What are the signs? Calmness, experience, thoughtfulness, seriousness, maturity, and heartfelt sincerity. These are also the qualities that give "persuasiveness to his lips." Whether someone gets his or her wisdom from education, experience, or old-fashioned thoughtfulness, when that wise heart guides his or her mouth, it's worthy of our full attention.

Thank God for people who constantly show us how to be thoughtful. They care for us, appreciate us, and encourage us. We call them friends, loved ones, and brothers. But—we must remember that we are being taught to teach! God has blessed us with wonderful examples so that we can become an example to others. There is no area of our life where this is more important than with our children. If there was ever a place where wisdom needs to guide our mouth it is when we talk with those precious souls that God entrusted to our care. If they don't learn to think before they speak from us, where are they going to learn it? We are the primary teachers and examples for our children. How sad it is when a child must overcome poor parental examples to be pleasing to God.

On the other hand, there is no greater joy than to see your children develop a Christlike thoughtfulness. I have experienced what Solomon wrote about when he said,

> My son, if your heart is wise,
> My own heart also will be glad;
> And my inmost being will rejoice
> When your lips speak what is right
> –Proverbs 23:15-16

At the time I am writing this all three of my children and my son-in-law are in college. I am so proud of them for all their accomplishments and honors, but what means the most to me is that they all love God and are committed to being like Jesus. I know that they are growing spiritually because they are becoming more and more Christlike. One of the best ways to determine that such growth is taking place is to see how thoughtful they have become. They are encouragers, givers, card senders, inspirers, listeners; sympathetic, caring, and loving. I truly care nothing about how that reflects on me. I'm just excited that they glorify God by having the kind of heart He wants them to have. To say my heart is glad is true, but it's also a serious understatement.

Think Before You Speak

That brings me to one final point about thoughtfulness: There's no such thing as too much! I've heard all my life that you can have too much of a good thing. That's not true when it comes to thoughtfulness. Thoughtfulness is not only thinking before talking, but also it's thinking about others instead of yourself. The more we do that the more we are being like Jesus! How could we possibly do too much of that? We are talking about something that is precious, beautiful, and life changing. Here's how Solomon described it:

> *Pleasant words are a honeycomb,*
> *Sweet to the soul and healing to the bones*
> —Proverbs 16:24

Even though it was against his father's wishes, Jonathan "put out the end of the staff that was in his hand and dipped it in the honeycomb, and put his hand to his mouth, and his eyes brightened" (1 Samuel 14:27). Pleasant words have the same effect. They lift the spirit, warm the soul, and bring emotional and physical healing to the recipient. What an amazing power that is! Power to touch souls! Power to change lives! Power to give comfort and hope! All because we took the time to think, chose to give, and made it sweet.

APPROPRIATE

Just as we learn from Jesus how important it is to think or be thoughtful before we speak, we also learn from Him that our words should be appropriate. He always knew what was the appropriate thing to say at any occasion. The religious leaders of His time were always trying to trick Him into saying something that would discredit Him with the people. They were never successful. When the time came to put Him on trial, they had to rely on twisted interpretations and outright lies.

The story of Jesus handling the crowd when they brought the adulterous woman to Him is probably the best-known example of His dealing with enemies with appropriate words. There's another example, however, that I like to think about whenever I reflect on Jesus' ability to say what needed to be said. He had recently driven the money changers and profiteers out of the temple, and His miracles were known far and wide. At this point in His ministry He had the popular support of the people, so He wasn't particularly concerned with what the religious leaders could do to Him.

The Bible says that He came to the temple and began to speak to the crowds. There were usually several rabbis and other teachers speaking at various places in the temple. Jesus, however, attracted large crowds and atten-

I Knew That!

tion because of the miracles He had performed and the power of His teachings. The chief priests and the elders decided to confront Him in front of the people and try to trick Him into saying something that would turn them against Him.

"By what authority," they asked, "are You doing these things, and who gave You this authority?" They wanted Him to publicly proclaim that He was the Messiah or a prophet of God, or some special spokesman from God. Then they could put Him on the defensive by demanding that He prove it. After all, they were the ones who spoke for God. Not this carpenter from the boonies, who was uneducated and obviously poor.

If it had been me and I had Jesus' power I would have shown them what kind of authority I had with one brief bolt of lightening that would have fried them where they stood. But Jesus didn't even answer their question. He made them a deal! He said in essence, If you answer My question I'll answer yours. That shouldn't have been too threatening for a bunch of religious scholars like them.

He asked, "The baptism of John was from what source, from heaven or from men?" Seemed simple enough, but as they huddled in discussion they realized that they had just been put in a no-win position by that country bumpkin. If they said John's baptism was from heaven, He would simply ask them why they didn't listen to him. On the other hand, if they said it was from men the crowds would turn against them since they considered John to be a prophet. They were stuck! So those pompous hypocrites had to grit their teeth and mumble, "We do not know." To which Jesus replied, "Neither will I tell you by what authority I do these things" (Matthew 21:23-27).

His words were more than clever and revealing, they were appropriate for the situation. They were also appropriate for the Son of God, who could look into the hearts and minds of religious hypocrites and catch them in their scheming. We don't have His ability, but we can have His spirit—a spirit that wants to please God and represent Him appropriately.

Solomon mentioned this on several occasions.

> *The lips of the righteous bring forth what is acceptable,*
> *But the mouth of the wicked what is perverted*
> –Proverbs 10:32

Acceptable to whom? Who decides what is acceptable when it comes to words? The obvious answer is God, but most of our communication is not with God! The point we must remember is: *All of our communication must be acceptable to Him even when we aren't talking to Him!*

The NIV uses the word "fitting" in place of the word "acceptable." I like that because it has us feeling appropriateness rather than judgment. Okay—so I'm a whimp! I like the image of a father nurturing his son with the admonition "Son, that was out of place," better than the disciplinarian with crossed arms declaring, "That was totally unacceptable!" The word fitting also doesn't let us off the hook when we have said things that were technically right, but not representative of Christ. Things that are spiritually out of place.

One of the ironies that I have pointed out in my books on worship, *Spilt Grape Juice* and *Unbroken Bread*, is that Christians become un-Christlike when we disagree on how Christ should be worshiped in our assemblies. I've heard Christians say, "I hate it when we do something different during the communion!" It wasn't that the elements, order, or focus were changed, it was some small change in the traditional way of doing it (i.e., before or after the sermon, a song between the bread and cup, or a dramatic reading of Scripture before, etc.). But to say, "I hate it" when we are talking about our Lord's love, sacrifice, and commitment to us? A spiritual feast that is all about fellowship, oneness, self-examination, agape, being cross-focused and second-coming prepared? It's technically okay to have a preference, but it's never correct to be ungodly in the way we express it! It's unfitting for a Christian!

One who has been declared righteous by God speaks what is fitting consistently. What is fitting consistently? What Jesus would say if He were in your shoes! After all, He is—isn't He? Because of that we must remember the "Least of These" principle from Matthew 25:31-46. He told us that what we did to one of the least of His brothers we did to Him. While He mentioned specific acts of love, the principle clearly applies to what crosses our lips.

You already know who's on the Least List in your life, but just in case you have forgotten, it includes the waitress, the janitor, the obnoxious coworker, the crazy drivers of rush hour, the store clerk with an attitude, the irritating phone salesperson, the referees at the ball game, the loud-mouthed competitors, your whining kids, your stressed-out spouse, the closed-minded traditionalist, the wild-eyed progressive, and—well, everyone else in the whole wide world that you might talk to.

Solomon gives us another angle to contemplate with two proverbs from chapter 15.

A man has joy in an apt answer,
And how delightful is a timely word!

–v. 23

I Knew That!

The heart of the righteous ponders how to answer,
But the mouth of the wicked pours out evil things.

—v. 28

These are both "Think before you speak" passages. An "apt answer" is not a quick answer, but an appropriate one. Verse 23 is classic Hebrew parallelism with the same thing being said twice, just differently. Apt and timely are used synonymously and refer to a well-thought-out response. What I like about Solomon's wisdom in these two proverbs is the personal satisfaction that one receives from doing something right. When we take the time to think things through and give a helpful, insightful, and intelligent answer, it's a joy and a delight.

It's because we want to be pleasing to God that we must take the time to think before we speak. "The heart of the righteous ponders" means that we recognize the importance of being appropriate, godly, and truthful. We represent God, so we must ponder from our hearts. The word ponder means to weigh, consider, meditate, or study.[2] Take your time! Think it through! Kneel down and write in the dirt! It's not so much a matter of being right or wrong as remembering that you can't take it back—so make it appropriate the first time.

It's no fun to dwell on the negative, but Solomon does point out that "the mouth of the wicked pours out evil things." I've been around people who had evil things pouring out of their mouths constantly. Sometimes it was nasty cursing that showed the individual to be linguistically challenged, and other times it was just ugly, hateful, and filthy. That's why I quit going to elders meetings! No—these were usually people being arrested by the police when I was a police chaplain. Some were indescribably evil. I remember drunks that we locked up for Driving While Intoxicated, who called me every name imaginable because I was helping to incarcerate them unjustly. I often wondered about the hearts of those people who were so evil when their inhibitions were down because of intoxication. They must have harbored a great deal of evil in their hearts to have it flow so freely when separated from social restraints. If it's in your heart, it can never be completely hidden.

I can't finish this study without taking a good look at the importance and beauty of "a timely word." A couple of weeks ago my wife and I were walking out to our vehicle in the church parking lot after our Sunday morning assemblies were over, and she called out to a sister who was also walking to her car. Donna called her name and simply told her how pretty she looked in the dress she had on. It was a simple thing to do and rather typical of my wife whom I accuse of having to be the last person to leave the church building every time.

Think Before You Speak

A few days later, Donna received a sweet card from that sister stating how much it meant to her that Donna knew her name and cared enough to give her a compliment. She went on to tell Donna that it really picked her up after a very difficult week. She was so appreciative for those few words of encouragement. But that's the lesson—it wasn't just the words, it was the timing of the words!

Oh that we could break out of our selfish shells and see opportunities to bless others with a timely word. Timely words change lives. How much of what we are today is due to the hundreds of people who gave us timely words? Remember the teachers, friends, family members, and even strangers who said, "Great job," "You've really got a talent," "You can do it," " I'm proud of you," "God has blessed you," "Have you ever thought about preaching (or whatever fits you)," "How do you know but that God put you here for just such a purpose as this?" "I understand what you're going through," and such like? That same power to change lives is in your hands now. A timely word spoken to a child, a teenager, a single, a young couple, a struggling Christian, a seeker of God, an elderly widow or widower, a beaten elder, a worn-out teacher, or just someone who could use it, could turn them around like you'd never expect.

A timely word is a thing of beauty. As Solomon declared:

> *Like apples of gold in settings of silver*
> *Is a word spoken in the right circumstances*
> –Proverbs 25:11

A well-thought-out word, spoken at just the right time, is a lovely, priceless, work of art. That's a pretty impressive gift to give to anybody. When you think about it though, the most precious gifts you've ever been given were words. What kind of value would you place on "I love you?" What can compare to the words, "I now baptize you in the name of the Father, the Son, and Holy Spirit, for the remission of your sins?" How important to you are the words "I now pronounce you husband and wife?" How much do you long to hear the words, "Well done, good and faithful slave. . . . enter into the joy of your master"?

A thing of beauty given at just the right time! Sounds unusually familiar to me. It sounds suspiciously like Jesus. "For while we were still helpless, at the right time Christ died for the ungodly" (Romans 5:6). If you find yourself saying, "Wait a second! I thought we were talking about words?" We are. Remember John 1:1, "In the beginning was the Word, and the Word was with God, and the Word was God." Maybe the key to all this is recognizing that everything we give, even our words, is a form of sharing Jesus. All the more reason we need to think before we speak.

CONTROLLED

This is obvious since our words will be neither thoughtful nor appropriate if we aren't controlled, but this is so essential that it needs to be a separate point. Controlled speech is purposeful. If we want to be thoughtful and appropriate we must be motivated and intentional. Let's face it, we all are tempted to react and say what first crosses our minds, but it's not what's best or what's Christlike. The secular world, especially secular counseling, tells us to "let it all go, say what you're thinking, and don't hold anything back." It's offered under the guise of "being real" and "being honest with yourself and others." It really is just giving in to urges, weaknesses, temptation, sin, and Satan.

No one would argue against being honest and real, but the higher priority is being like Jesus. The Bible tells us that we should be "speaking the truth in love" (Ephesians 4:15), but that is not license to spew out whatever crosses our minds. Honest communication, or "speaking the truth in love," is the key to building every relationship, but it must be controlled, guided, and dominated by our passion for being Christlike. In the same passage where we are told to speak the truth in love, Paul also said, " be renewed in the spirit of your mind, and put on the new self, which in the likeness of God has been created in righteousness and holiness of truth." He then makes another plea for us to be truthful with one another, but adds, "BE ANGRY, AND yet DO NOT SIN; do not let the sun go down on your anger, and do not give the devil an opportunity" (Ephesians 4:26-27).

Paul is talking about the need for self-control in our actions and our speech. Don't give in to the urge to be controlled by your anger. What we say in anger will rarely be representative of Jesus and will nearly always "give the devil an opportunity." It's easy to give in to temptations in the name of being truthful when *the* truth is we've lost control. How many ungodly things have been done in the name of "I'm just being honest?" How many times have people been ruthless, unkind, uncaring, and un-like Jesus, and called it "just being truthful?"

We are "a living sacrifice" to God, which means that you and I must live a life of worship to Him (Romans 12:1). Jesus made it clear that in the New Covenant, those who wanted to worship God must worship Him, not at a place or time, but "in spirit and truth" (John 4:21-24). There must be truth, but truth without spirit is unacceptable to God. Because we are guided by spirit as well as truth, that spirit controls the attitude and appropriateness of what we say. No other passage of Scripture, in my opinion, reveals this godly control more than the closing verses of Ephesians chapter 4. The clash of who or what controls our speech is clearly delineated. Read this slowly:

> *Let no unwholesome word proceed from your mouth, but only such a word as is good for edification according to the need of the moment, that it may give grace to those who hear. Do not grieve the Holy Spirit of God, by whom you were sealed for the day of redemption. Let all bitterness and wrath and anger and clamor and slander be put away from you, along with all malice. Be kind to one another, tender-hearted, forgiving each other, just as God in Christ also has forgiven you.*
> –vv. 29-32

Doesn't this passage just scream the message that we must control our speech with the love of Christ? Truth must be guided by wholesomeness, edification, grace, kindness, compassion, forgiveness, and by Jesus. If we give in to the urge to be guided by the negative list in that passage, we've chosen Satan over God.

Solomon was heavy on the practical side of this issue. His words of wisdom about controlling our speech have the ring of common sense to them. It's smart to use control when we speak, even if we were not concerned with pleasing God (which we very much are—right?). As Solomon said,

> *The one who guards his mouth preserves his life;*
> *The one who opens wide his lips comes to ruin*
> –Proverbs 13:3

Think before you speak because it could save your life! When I was a preteen, I nearly got my older brother and me killed one night. We were walking home from a late movie in the dead of winter with several inches of snow on the ground. There were four of us—another brother team, the same ages as my brother and I. We were having a grand time sliding, pushing each other, and generally whooping it up. At one point a carload of older guys (still young, but older than us), came zooming by yelling obscene things at us. Well, with a buddy there and two older brothers, I felt invincible, so I proceeded to shout something inappropriate and utterly stupid back at them. The car skidded to a stop and started to back up. In response, we ran for our lives.

The long version is even scarier, but the short version is that the two older brothers, mine and my friend's, were caught and beat up by the carload of

I Knew That!

road warriors. They caught me too, but decided I was too young to have shouted nasty things at them, and they let me go. Needless to say, my brother, who to his credit was actually able to laugh about it, regularly reminded me to keep my mouth shut when people in passing cars yelled at us.

I like the idea of guarding our mouths. We guard what we put in them, especially if it doesn't taste good. It must be clean, and not too sweet, or too sour, or too much. We brush our teeth, use mouthwash, and make regular trips to the dentist, all to guard against tooth decay or some other problem in our mouths. Yet we do little or nothing to guard what comes out of our mouths. We have to rely on experience (hard knocks), social acceptability, and common sense. Any or all of these may be deficient in a person's life. Saying what Jesus would say, on any given occasion, is always appropriate. There's no guarantee that it will preserve one's life, but it will certainly keep us controlled, thoughtful, and appropriate.

The next passage from Proverbs is very well known, and is perfectly illustrated by Jesus in the way He dealt with the crowd wanting to stone the woman caught adultery. Solomon said,

> *A gentle answer turns away wrath,*
> *But a harsh word stirs up anger.*
>
> –Proverbs 15:1

Jesus proved that a bloodthirsty mob can be transformed by "a gentle answer," but you and I will probably never face such a situation. We have something tougher to deal with—kids. There's no place in our lives where it's more important to control the urge to react than when we are dealing with our children. How sad it is that children have to overcome parental examples to learn the art of gentleness. Our lives are so stress filled, competitive, and anxious that we've used up our supply of patience and kindness by the time we get to be with our kids. So we explode, yell, snip, ridicule, and demand! We react to their immaturity with our immaturity and wonder why they never learn to accept responsibility! We contribute to, and even start, the cycle of anger in our families because we don't value gentleness enough.

I know parents who scream and rant at their children over any point of dissatisfaction. The kids either learn to ignore it or they turn into frightened prisoners who duck every time dad scratches his head. Either way, resentment and anger grow and it contributes to everything from dysfunctional families to homicidal maniacs.

It's such a powerful principle, so true, yet so forgotten! "A gentle answer turns away wrath." Parents need to model this behavior for their children. Teachers need to show this to their students. Kids don't have the control button of your emotions unless you let them have it. Refuse to react and choose to relax. Think about what Jesus would say. You know that He would say something gentle and kind because "a harsh word stirs up anger," and Jesus is not in the anger business.

Take time to think it through. One day your children will realize that you showed them how to be Christlike, and they will thank you for it. Show them that it's important for all of us to keep our words under control.

Maybe it's time to let controlled, appropriate, and thoughtful behavior at home influence the way we act at work, instead of letting out-of-control, inappropriate, and thoughtless behavior at work influence our home lives. Deciding to give "a gentle answer" may be the ultimate think-before-you-speak example. Break the pattern of "harsh words" in all your interactions. When you do that you break the cycle of anger, dissatisfaction, and disappointment with yourself. You will be amazed at how differently others react to you. It's smart, it's productive, it's exemplary, and it's Christlike.

I especially like the way Solomon put it in Proverbs 17:27-28:

> *He who restrains his words has knowledge,*
> *And he who has a cool spirit is a man of understanding.*
> *Even a fool, when he keeps silent, is considered wise;*
> *When he closes his lips, he is counted prudent.*

Be cool! Watch your words! People may think you're smart, so don't open your mouth and prove them wrong!

A RESTRAINED CONCLUSION

Have you ever thought about Jesus having to control Himself? Before you shout, "Blasphemy!" remember the Bible tells us that Jesus is able to "sympathize with our weaknesses" because He "has been tempted in all things as we are, yet without sin" (Hebrews 4:15). What is temptation if it isn't the presentation of an evil option to any given situation? If Jesus was tempted in every way we are, that means He had to have been tempted to lose control, get angry, react, or just generally give someone a piece of His mind. He certainly had the opportunity—and most of us would say He had the justification! His enemies were goading Him! Trying to get Him to get irked and say something the Son of God would never say! Yet He never reacted, retaliated, or was ruled by anger. He was never guided by the stress others imposed on Him or that He

I Knew That!

imposed on Himself! He said things that were thoughtful, appropriate, and controlled (meaning He didn't give in to the temptation to lose control).

Even while on the cross, He never let the circumstances dictate His behavior. He thought about His mother and her future. He gave hope to a fellow victim. He gave forgiveness to His killers.

They were not supernatural words from a supernatural being. They were simple, heartfelt words from a very human Savior who showed us how to walk and talk, and how to die and live again.

NOTES
1. Tan, Paul Lee, *Encyclopedia of 7700 Illustrations: Signs of the Times* (Rockville, MD: Assurance Publishers, 1979), pp. 1435-1437.
2. "Proverbs," *The Expositor's Bible Commentary*, vol. 5), p. 1000.

CHAPTER SIX
"Honesty Is the Best Policy"

Years ago, a famous preacher decided to preach to his large audience about honesty. He used the story of Ananias and Sapphira in Acts 5 as his text. As you remember, they told a lie about their giving and God struck them dead. The old preacher declared, "God doesn't strike people dead for lying like He used to. If He did, where would I be?" He paused while the audience snickered a bit. Then he roared, "I tell you where I would be. I would be right here preaching to an empty house!"[1]

It's safe to say that one of the earliest lessons any of us learned is "Honesty is the best policy." We've known that all our lives, yet it's one of those principles of living that we regularly forget. How many times have you slapped yourself on the forehead and said, "I knew that" about honesty? It's one of the earliest temptations we face in life. Mom or dad confront us about something that's missing, moved, or had unauthorized child tampering, and we think, "What's the best way to avoid punishment?" The brain quickly suggests—"lie for all your worth!" We do; it works. We learn for the first time: If it saves you some pain and makes you look good, give lying a chance!

Of course, we didn't always get away with it. There were plenty of times when we lied or were otherwise dishonest and we got caught. We were embarrassed, humiliated, sorely penitent, and we vowed to always be honest from that moment on. And we were—until the next time.

The temptation to be dishonest is arguably the most pervasive temptation in life. We don't like admitting to mistakes. We don't want to look bad to people. We don't like getting caught. Lying is almost a natural defense mechanism for life! Add to that the offensive elements of self-promotion, exaggeration, attention getting, and impressing others, and you have plenty of motivation to be dishonest. Here are a few classic temptations to lie:

I Knew That!

"Why are you late?"
"Where's your homework?"
"Who left the door open?"
"Did I give you too much change?"
"Did you run all your laps?"
"Don't you owe me some money?"
"Everything on this tax form is true, right?"
"Are those reports finished yet?"
"Where have you been?"
"Hey, Dad. Did you ever _____?"
"You know that story in Luke 8?"
"Is your heart right with God?"
"Can I see your license please. Do you know how fast you were going?"
"Have you prayed today?"
"Do you have a dollar I can borrow?"
"I'm calling on behalf of Acme Vinyl Siding. Is Michael R. Root at home?"

Obviously the list is endless. Sometimes it's difficult to identify dishonesty because it comes in so many different forms, colors, and shades. Some of which we don't even think of as being wrong. A lie or a falsehood automatically sounds bad, but what about an untruth? How about misrepresentation, invention, exaggeration, equivocation, distortion, evasion, imitation, deception, duplicity, pretense, or concealment? Then there is misstating, misquoting, misreporting, misinforming, misleading, fabricating, forging, concocting, coloring, and slanting. Check out your thesaurus and look at all the slang words and phrases we have to describe someone who is not telling the truth.

We can even be dishonest for what we think are good reasons, like pretending or having fun. Are we lying when we tell our children about Santa Claus or the Easter Bunny? What if you attend a Halloween party in full costume and spend the evening pretending to be Luke Skywalker? Honesty is a condition of the heart. God is not concerned with our good-natured joking or pretending. He is concerned when we don't care about truth, integrity, and being Christlike.

Even well-intentioned "exaggerations" can backfire on us. I like the story about Mrs. Brown who was appalled when her little boy told a blatant lie. She sat him down immediately and had a serious talk with him. She warned him that "when little boys tell lies, a huge dark man with fiery red eyes and two sharp horns snatches them up and takes them to Mars where they have to work in dark mines for fifty years! So," she concluded, "you won't tell

Honesty Is the Best Policy

another lie ever again will you?"

"Why no, Mom," said the boy seriously. "You tell better ones."

Few things are more embarrassing than being caught in a lie. You probably remember a time as a child when that happened and it probably still makes your stomach tie up in knots just thinking about it. On the other hand, there are few things more painful than to be thought of as lying when you are telling the truth. As a youngster, I took a dollar from my older brother's paper route money and spent it on candy. When my mother confronted me about it later, I lied like crazy, but guilt was written all over my face. A few months later, another dollar was missing from my mother's dresser and I was accused of taking it. I hadn't, but I couldn't convince anyone that I was innocent. I later found out that a friend of mine, who was waiting on me to change my clothes so we could go play together, took it. To this day, I remember both incidents well, and I'm still not sure which one was worse. I am sure, however, that honesty is the best policy.

Not only is honesty the best policy, but it may also be the best indicator of the depth of our integrity. There is no integrity without honesty. Integrity is consistent character. It's what we are when no one is looking. Integrity is, I think, being consistently honest—honest with God, others, and yourself. Honesty is a way of life! It's being honest when no one but you and God know what happened. I mention it often, but my favorite definition of integrity is that it's the gift you give yourself. Isn't that what honesty is all about? Giving yourself a guilt-free conscience, feeling good about doing what's right, and knowing that God is smiling at your heart.

Our nation was built by men and women who valued honesty. Thomas Jefferson once said, "The whole art of government consists in the art of being honest." That's certainly relevant today with a sitting President who told the nation he "hadn't been totally accurate" in describing his Oval Office activities with a certain intern. It seems that many politicians believe that the best policy is what gets you elected and that doesn't include honesty.

Benjamin Franklin concluded, "An honest man will receive neither money nor praise that is not his due." The pursuit of money and power has been the source of incredible dishonesty from televangelists to office seekers, and from living rooms to boardrooms. The belief is that the end justifies the means, but the end is just as misplaced as the means is wrong. As one poet summed it up,

I Knew That!

> *It matters not what you do—*
> *Make a nation or a shoe;*
> *For he who does an honest thing*
> *In God's pure sight is ranked a king.*
>
> —John Parnell[2]

Most people know that Jesus' parable of the sower in Luke 8 is really not about the sower but the soils in which he sows seed. Most people also know that the four different soils represent four different kinds of hearts. He sowed seed on the roadside, and it was trampled by travelers and eaten by birds. Then he spread some seed on rocky soil, which sprang up, but died out because of no moisture. Some of his seed fell among the thorns and grew initially, but it was choked out by the overpowering thorns. The seed that fell on the good soil grew and produced a huge crop.

The seed symbolizes the Word of God and the point of the parable is how different hearts receive that seed. The roadside heart is weak and it allows the devil to snatch the seed away. The rock heart receives it with excitement but it doesn't have deep roots so it withers and dies. The thorny heart also receives the seed with enthusiasm, but "as they go on their way they are choked with worries and riches and pleasures of this life, and bring no fruit to maturity."

The pursuit of riches and pleasures chokes the honesty, integrity, and even the life right out of us. You might be saying, "He's not talking about honesty!" Are you sure? Listen to Jesus' description of what made the good soil so good.

> But the seed in the good soil, these are the ones who have heard the word in an honest and good heart, and hold it fast, and bear fruit with perseverance.
>
> —v. 15

Jesus was proclaiming that His Word will only be able to truly germinate and grow in a heart that is honest and good. He didn't say perfect or sinless. An honest heart will recognize sin and do something to remove it. A dishonest heart will ignore sin, be unrepentant, and rationalize it away. An honest heart can be touched, broken, convicted, and most importantly, healed. An honest heart is a humble heart, and as we've pointed out previously, "God opposes the proud, but gives grace to the humble." So the honest heart has God on its side.

When you stop and realize that in the Bible honesty includes anything concerning truth, truthfulness, goodness, just, right, righteous, sincerity,

Honesty Is the Best Policy

uprightness, and the like, you begin to understand that it permeates the Word. Honesty is a foundational and fundamental element of our becoming what God wants us to be. Honesty is truth! It's the essence of godliness because God is the source of all truth. It's being Christlike since Jesus is "the truth" (John 14:6). It's the way we worship God, who must be worshiped "in spirit and truth" (John 4:24). It's truth that sanctifies us and truth that sets us free (John 8:32 and John 17:17).

I've heard many debates and arguments over what is essential to our salvation. I've never heard anyone question the essentiality of honesty. If honesty is optional, so is truth. It's not the *best* policy! For Christians it's the *only* policy!

A DECEITFUL HEART

I wonder how Solomon felt about being a child of deceit? By the time he became king of Israel the story of David and Bathsheba was part of the national heritage. It was a story that was told to children, taught in the temple, and immortalized by scribes. He had heard it all his life and he knew that everyone else knew the story, too.

I suspect that Solomon's perspective on his dad's best-known sin, was different than what we might think it would be. Because of our cultural evaluation of sins, with some being big sins while others are just little, and because of our preoccupation with sex, we tend to think of David's adultery. We think, "He was unfaithful! He lusted and had sexual relations with another man's wife! He was guilty of adultery!" Our perspective is severely colored by our Victorian heritage and Puritan roots. David was already a polygamist. He was the king and what the king wanted the king got! I wouldn't be surprised if there had been plenty of illicit assignations between David and women he was attracted to. Maybe not, but the point I want to make is that Solomon, who had a thousand women to keep track of, wouldn't have been as concerned about his father's sexual indiscretion as much as he would his efforts to cover it up—his deceit.

David went to some serious extremes to cover up Bathsheba's pregnancy. He had his men lie to Uriah, Bathsheba's husband, about why he needed to leave his men and the battle to meet the king. He lied to Uriah. He acted like he cared about how the war was going. He acted like he was interested in Uriah getting some R & R, when in reality he was wanting him to go home and have a conjugal visit with his wife and thus be deceived into believing that the baby would be his. David even got him drunk, thinking surely that would do the trick, but Uriah was a man of integrity and he refused to enjoy pleasures that his men on the battlefield couldn't enjoy.

I Knew That!

When all other forms of deception failed, David arranged for Uriah to be placed in a battle hot spot where he would certainly be killed. When the traditional period of mourning was over for Bathsheba, she immediately became another one of David's wives. The baby she bore him became sick and died. He was the son who would have been king of Israel instead of Solomon. That's another reason his perspective was different from ours and it helps explain why some of his proverbs have such a personal ring to them (2 Samuel 11 and 12).

The following is inspiration, but it's also the voice of experience.

> *Truthful lips will be established forever,*
> *But a lying tongue is only for a moment.*
> *Deceit is in the heart of those who devise evil,*
> *But counselors of peace have joy.*
> *No harm befalls the righteous,*
> *But the wicked are filled with trouble.*
> *Lying lips are an abomination to the LORD,*
> *But those who deal faithfully are His delight*
> —Proverbs 12:19-22

The word honesty doesn't even appear in this passage once, but it screams honesty on nearly every line. Truthful lips are the opposite of lying tongues; deceit is the opposite of joy; righteous is the opposite of wicked; and lying lips are the opposite of being faithful. Truth and honesty last forever, generate peace, and are a delight to God. Lying and dishonesty are soon discovered, evil, filled with trouble, and are an abomination to God. It would be hard to find a clearer contrast anywhere in the Bible than what Solomon wrote here.

The most thought-provoking phrase in the passage is "Deceit is in the heart." The one who would "devise evil" must think about it, plan, and have a cold, insensitive heart. This passage is actually making a contrast between those who plot evil and those who promote peace.[3] The evil plotter will cause and receive pain and sorrow, while the "counselors of peace" have joy and contentment. Why would someone want to plan evil things? Especially when it produces so many negative results. It doesn't make any sense unless you understand that the problem is the heart not the logic.

Is honesty really the best policy? God says it is! If truth, joy, security, and pleasing God are important to us, choosing honesty is clearly best. If we want people to be pleased with us more than we want God to be pleased with us, we will inevitably give into the temptation to deceive. The desire to be

Honesty Is the Best Policy

admired and accepted by others is a powerful driving force in our lives. Just look at the things we do that are, for all practical purposes, culturally acceptable deceptions.

Do you wake up in the morning looking the same as you do by the time you get to work? Are you really everything you appear to be? Is your house always as clean as when company comes over? Is your family, your marriage, and your personal life as "all together" as it looks when you walk into the church building on Sunday morning? How many kinds and forms of culturally acceptable deception do you think we have? What are some of the possibilities? Make up? Whigs? Girdles? Shoe lifts? Tinted contact lenses? Hair dye? Cosmetic surgery? Dental work? Impressive luxury car? Youthful looking sports car? Professional-looking, religious-looking, or expensive-looking attire? Carrying a briefcase, a laptop, a Bible?

How much of a leap is it to go from culturally acceptable deceit to ungodly deceit? It may not be far, but the difference is in the condition of the heart. The heart that is full of deceit and plots to do evil is a heart that follows Satan not God. That is why He detests "lying lips." A heart that is given over to sin, where planning evil and being dishonest is normal, is a very sad sight to God. I've used them a lot to illustrate various points, but Ananias and his wife Sapphira are excellent examples of how God feels about deceit. They were not struck dead by God because they only gave part of their land-sale money to the church. They were punished because, as Peter said, "Satan **filled your heart** to lie to the Holy Spirit." He later asked, "Why is it that you have **conceived this deed in your heart**? You have not lied to men, but to God" (Acts 5:1-11, emphasis added). Their sin was having a dishonest and deceitful heart.

If Ananias and Sapphira could speak to us today I'm sure they would tell us that honesty truly is the best policy. But we don't need them to tell us that, when we have the Holy Spirit telling us the exact same thing nearly every page of the Bible.

A RIGHTEOUS HATRED

How many kindly mothers and grandmothers have rebuked a child for saying they hated something with, "Now don't say 'hate.' A Christian must never hate"? Is that right? Do Christians ever hate? Sure they do! They must! The problem is not the word hate, but what we mean when we use it. That is true even in the way the word is used in Scripture.

Many, if not most, of the times the Bible refers to hate, it is not used for literal hatred, but a dislike for or need to avoid particular things and people. For example, we are told to "hate the evil, and love the good," in Amos 5:10.

I Knew That!

The Psalmist said, "you that love the L<small>ORD</small> hate evil" (Psalm 89:32). What preacher is there among us who hasn't preached a sermon on the "six things which the L<small>ORD</small> hates," from Proverbs 6:16-19? Part of our struggle with sin comes from our inability to hate or strongly dislike it. If it weren't attractive and pleasurable we'd have no problem avoiding it.

The Bible also uses the word hate to describe a lesser degree of love. That is what Jesus was talking about when He declared that each of us have to "hate his own father and mother and wife and children and brothers and sisters, and even his own life," to be His disciple (Luke 14:26). That is not literal hatred, but merely a strong way of saying that He must come first in our lives.

If we don't recognize these differences in the use of the word hate we will have Jesus contradict His commanding us never to hate. The hatred that we must not allow into our hearts is enmity, bitterness, revenge, and loathing. Jesus said in the Sermon on the Mount that the old adage "Y<small>OU SHALL LOVE YOUR NEIGHBOR</small> and hate your enemy" is wrong! Those who have a Christlike spirit must "love your enemies, and pray for those who persecute you in order that you may be sons of your Father who is in heaven" (Matthew 5:43-45).

John, the apostle of love, made an even stronger statement in his first letter. He said, "Every one who hates his brother is a murderer; and you know that no murderer has eternal life abiding in him (1 John 3:15). You won't find a clearer declaration in the Bible of who will not go to heaven. This kind of hatred is the antithesis of what the spirit of Christ is all about. So when it comes to this use of the word hate, like grandma said, "A Christian must never say hate" or feel it if it's the ungodly kind of hate.

Now that we've done the word study, let's make the point. As children of God, there are things that we must be passionate about. Some things we love and some things we hate (strongly dislike). We need to have a passionate love for honesty, but also a passionate dislike for dishonesty. We must *care* and *care deeply*! Solomon said,

> *A righteous man hates falsehood,*
> *But a wicked man acts disgustingly and shamefully*
> –Proverbs 13:5

How do you feel about falsehoods, lies, or dishonesty? It is somewhat hard to be too passionate about hating falsehoods when we use them ourselves.

"A righteous man" is a person who is interested in pleasing God. That may not sound deeply theological, but if we are declared righteous because of our faith (Romans 4:3), and if faith is what pleases God (Hebrews 11:6), it's certainly safe to conclude that if a person is righteous, it means he is pleasing to God. This is Solomon's premise. The individual who is interested in pleasing God *will* hate falsehood!

Oops! (That's a technical term for "Do you realize what that means?") If we don't have a passionate dislike for falsehood, maybe it's because pleasing God isn't that important to us. If I were to ask you if you hated falsehood, you'd quickly respond, "Well of course I do!" But what if I asked you why? Do you hate falsehoods because of all the inconvenience they cause, all the hurt you've felt and given, and because of all the sin they generate? After all, "Honesty is the best policy," right? Honesty works best. It's efficient. It causes fewer problems. What about hating falsehood because God hates it and we want to be pleasing to Him?

It's because we are passionate about loving Him that we are passionate about hating falsehood. It's foreign to the spirit of God! He is Truth! To be passionate about Him is to be passionate about truth, which means we must be passionate about anything that destroys truth. Just as we "hunger and thirst for righteousness" (Matthew 5:6), we must hunger and thirst for honesty!

Solomon offers an interesting contrast between the righteous person who hates falsehood and the wicked who "acts disgustingly and shamefully." In the Hebrew, Solomon could be making a play on words. The root words for shame and disgust can mean "to spread the smell of scandal." The idea being that the wicked stink with lies and they spread that odor on even those they lie about.[4] While the righteous offer up to God the sweet fragrance of truth, the wicked spread the stink of falsehoods on everyone.

Not only is honesty the best policy, but it's also one of God's favorite smells!

A KISS ON THE LIPS

Most people are fully aware of the drama behind the great Helen Keller. If for no other reason than they saw the play or the movie of her transformation under the training of Anne Sullivan. Anne taught Helen how to overcome her seemingly insurmountable handicaps of no seeing, no hearing, and no speaking. She helped Helen rise to international renown and become a hero of history. They were inseparable friends for forty-nine years.

What most people don't know is that later in life, Anne Sullivan became totally blind herself. Helen Keller then became her teacher and lovingly helped her overcome her loss of sight. They remained best friends until Anne's death. At her bedside, Helen said, "I pray for strength to endure the silent dark until she smiles upon me again."[5]

I love stories of friendship, don't you? The very essence of true friendship incorporates things like love, loyalty, sacrifice, and sharing. That's what we all want! We want friends who will care about us as much as we care about them. We want someone we can depend on and who will love us in spite of our weaknesses. We want friends we can call at 2:00 A.M. and ask for help, and know we'll get it. But—we also want friends who will be honest with us.

Honesty is an assumed element in good relationships. We don't even think about it being a requirement, but we all know there can be no long-lasting, viable, and growing relationship if we don't give and receive the truth. In fact, the depth of our relationships is usually measured by the level of honesty that exists in them. Because we care, we want honesty in our relationships. The loss of honesty is usually an obvious sign of deterioration in the relationship. So, in a very real sense, honesty is an act of love.

Solomon gave us a very poignant picture of this point in Proverbs 24:26.

An honest answer is like a kiss on the lips.
−NIV

When I read this I thought, "Wow! I never realized that honesty could be such a passionate thing!" It seemed obvious to me that Solomon was trying to appeal to all the male readers of Proverbs. The logic being something like this: If you could receive a kiss from a beautiful woman, would you rather have a little peck on the cheek or a big passionate kiss right on the lips? Well, that's how much better an honest answer is!

Sounds good, but while the conclusion is right, the gender specificity is wrong. The mental pictures I conjured up are culturally biased. In the culture of that day, as it still is in many eastern countries, a kiss was a sign of friendship. As much as it may repulse most American males today, back then, a kiss on the lips was a sign of true friendship. It signified that the relationship was special—something people desired since close friendships were considered real treasures. The New American Standard Bible words it this way:

He kisses the lips
Who gives a right answer.

The point being, an honest or truthful answer is a mark of close friendship.[6]

I have already discussed the value of honesty and how we should have a passion for honesty, but just take a moment to reflect on how important it is to the relationships you care about. What kind of marriage can you have if it's not based on honesty? Who do you go to for an honest appraisal or evaluation if

Honesty Is the Best Policy

not your friends? How can you have a life-long relationship with your children if it's built on dishonesty? How can you respect a God who ignores your disdain for the truth? How can you treasure His Word if it's not totally honest?

In recent years the WWJD logo has been en vogue. The question, "What would Jesus do?" has been around since He challenged His disciples to "take up your cross and follow Me." Yet, as old as it is—even to the point of being a cliché, it is the essence of spiritual consistency. Jesus would be honest. In fact, He couldn't be dishonest. He'd never lie to anyone, be they family, friends, or a Roman Governor deciding whether He should live or die. You and I are truly being Christlike when we are totally—consistently honest.

Just think about what that means! We tend to think that being Christlike means that we are kind, compassionate, sacrificial, and humble. That's true of course, but we can do all those things for selfish reasons. We could be dishonest about acting like Jesus and we could be dishonest about what we say. Maybe the best way to build consistency in our lives, at least in terms of people seeing Jesus living in us, is to be honest and open in all our communicating. If we are completely honest in all we say, we don't have any need to deceive, cover-up, or lie to others. Our actions will naturally follow suit. That's real love; that's what builds relationships; and that's what spiritual integrity is all about. To the recipient—it's like a kiss on the lips.

I WAS ONLY JOKING!

How often do we hide truth behind the smoke screen of humor? Have you ever made fun of an overweight person and deflected the unkindness with, "I was just joking"? Have you ever excused racial slurs, sexual innuendoes, criticism, and derogatory remarks with "I was just kidding"? How many times have you vented your true feelings in the name of joking and being funny?

When I was a youngster growing up in southeast Washington, D.C., you could let someone get away with all kinds of jokes or cuts about you because, after all—it was all in fun. But, you never let someone insult your mother. A joke about your mother was an instant challenge to your manhood. They were fighting words. Saying, "I was only joking" just didn't change things either. There was either an apology or a fight—no two ways about it, because "my mother" was someone you didn't joke about.

The other day I saw a T-shirt that proclaimed, "Your mother is so dumb she stared at a carton of orange juice for twenty minutes because it said 'Concentrate'." I can only assume that "I'm only joking" was implied in the message and the wearer thought that was good enough to take away the offensive nature of the tasteless joke. Either that or he was a person who had no particular aspirations for longevity of life. I had interesting mental pictures of him explaining "the joke" to a large Hell's Angels gang.

Solomon offers us a graphic description of this kind of dishonesty.

> *Like a madman shooting*
> *firebrands or deadly arrows*
> *is a man who deceives his neighbor*
> *and says, "I was only joking!"*
> —Proverbs 26:18-19 NIV

Since I have been involved in archery for the last twenty years, this proverb is especially meaningful to me. So many people think of toy bows and arrows from their childhood when they think of archery that it's hard for many to realize how dangerous and lethal they are. They see a little wooden bow with rubber-tipped arrows and think, "What's the big deal? I shot my little brother with one of those things and he barely got a bruise from it."

Many of the great battles of history were won by efficient archers, who dispatched their opponents from staggering distances, and sometimes pierced thick armor plating. I have, on several occasions, seen one of my well-placed arrows zip through a large game animal like the proverbial hot knife through butter. I know how incredibly dangerous they can be. The blades of a broadhead are scalpel sharp. I've cut my fingers many times while just changing the blades. I can't image how dangerous a firebrand, or flaming arrow might be. It is because they are so dangerous that you simply don't play with them.

To shoot someone with an arrow or set them or their property on fire with a firebrand, is serious stuff! Only a crazy person would do such a thing and then wave it off with, "I was only joking!" Can you see your neighbor stumbling around with an arrow sticking from his chest and your saying, "Sorry, I was just kidding!"?

The use of the word madman is a strong word. It's not the same as "practical joker." This person is irresponsible, incompetent, and immature. One does not joke about such serious matters. God is saying that deception and dishonesty are that serious. It's nothing to joke about. Yet we still think we tell only "little white lies" and really only "stretch the truth." Dishonesty hurts people! It hurts both the dishonest person and the ones lied to or deceived.

It may not seem so bad at the time because it temporarily helps us avoid some kind of pain or other consequence, but eventually everyone suffers because truth was sacrificed on the altar of convenience. Dishonesty always hurts. It's one of Satan's least-appreciated weapons. As Solomon said,

Honesty Is the Best Policy

*Like a club and a sword and a sharp arrow
Is a man who bears false witness against his neighbor*
—Proverbs 25:18

The prophet of God stood before the king and condemned him for his idolatry. When the king stretched forth his hand pointing at the prophet and yelled, "Seize him," his hand withered up and became useless. God then caused the altar to split down the middle and all the ashes on it were poured out, just like the prophet had said it would. The king was shaken and contrite. He begged the man of God to pray for him that God would restore his hand. He did and God restored his hand to normal. The king was ready to give half his kingdom to the prophet, but he'd been commanded by God to return home. The command had been very specific. He was not to return by the same way he had come, and he was to abstain from food or drink until he got home. So he rejected the king's offer of fortune and food, and began his journey home.

Another man, who is simply described as "an old prophet," heard about all that the man of God had done and he went out and met him on the road. He suggested that the man of God come to his house for a meal, but that was a violation of God's command in that it would mean traveling on the route he took before, and it would violate the command to fast. He told the old prophet what God commanded, and the old prophet said, "I also am a prophet like you, and an angel spoke to me by the word of the LORD, saying, 'Bring him back with you to your house, that he may eat bread and drink water." The critical part of the story is the next phrase, "But he lied to him."

The man of God, believing the old prophet's story, went with him to his house and ate a meal. It turned out to be his last meal. Because he had violated God's command, he was killed by a lion and his body was thrown in the road for all to witness.

I don't understand everything about this story in 1 Kings 13, but I clearly see the lesson about the pain of dishonesty. The old prophet who lied might just as well have hit him with a club, stabbed him with a sword, or shot him with an arrow. His lies destroyed a man who had done some incredible things as God's spokesman. His deception was deadly for the man of God, and even though the story doesn't say anything about his punishment for lying, we know it wasn't overlooked. As Solomon declared, "**A false witness will not go unpunished, And he who tells lies will perish**" (Proverbs 19:9, emphasis added).

I Knew That!

HONEST TO GOD—I KNEW THAT!

We've looked at honesty from several different directions. Hopefully we understand that it is much bigger and far more important than we thought it was. Just in case that point has eluded you, chew on this question a little while. What is the connection between honesty and love?

The old song we sang when I was a youngster said that love and marriage go together like a horse and carriage. How does love and honesty go together? Are they interdependent? Can you have one and not the other and it remain the real thing?

Can you love God and not be honest with Him? We think we can. We ignore the fact that He knows exactly what is in our hearts. We continue to believe that if others think we are faithful and obedient then we must be faithful and obedient, regardless what our hearts tell us. We are church-going, Bible-carrying, directory-included, theologically correct, check-giving, meal-praying, long-standing members of the church. God knows it and He will reward us one day for being so . . . so . . . so . . . religious.

We need to sit on the seashore with Jesus and have Him give us the honesty test like He did Peter. "Do you love Me?" He asks. That's like asking a personal question in a Bible class. You'll always get a spiritual answer there because it's expected. "Of course I love You, Jesus!"

"Wait a second," He says. "I said do you *agape* Me? That means do you love Me the way that I love you, with agape love—unselfish and sacrificial?" Oh, it's a theological question. "Yes Lord, you know I agape you. I understand the truth. I know my Bible. I do the church thing all the time. I'm even a leader with a title."

With bowed head and tear-filled eyes He asks, "Do you love Me?"

Oh no! My theology is off. "Lord, you are my favorite Savior. I can't think of anyone I respect and admire more than You. You are the Great Teacher, the Head of the church, and the only Son of God. Of course I love You! I remember You every Sunday morning during the communion. I sing about You and I talk about You with all my church friends. I support Your church financially, which shows that my heart is in the right place. I don't drink, smoke, cuss, dance, or cheat on my wife. I . . . I . . . I . . . Why are you crying?"

He looks up with deepening lines of sadness on His face and asks, "Will you be My friend?"

As He looks into the depth of our hearts, He sees what we refuse to see. What we think is a deep, loving relationship is really just a passing acquaintance. We define ourselves by what we don't do rather than Who we are like. Instead of becoming more like Him, because of our long life-changing walk

Honesty Is the Best Policy

with Him, we are prideful and self-righteous because of how religious we are. We compare ourselves to others and feel smug when we should be comparing ourselves to Him and feeling broken and unworthy.

After Peter responded to each of Jesus' questions about loving Him, Jesus then challenged him, each time, to take care of His sheep. That seemed strange to me for a lot of years, until I asked myself the question, "How do we love Jesus?" We don't give Him a big hug or holy kiss and say, "I love you so much!" We don't send Him Hallmark cards or a huge arrangement of flowers. What can, and should, we do for God to show we love Him? We do what He has always asked us to do! The one consistent thing that demonstrates that He has made a difference in our lives! We love others! (Read John 13:34-35; 15:12-14; 1 John 3:23; 4:17-21.)

How does all this tie into honesty? Simple! There is no love for God without love for one another! We can say we love Him, we can feel like we love Him, everyone else can proclaim and believe that we love Him, *but* if we don't love our neighbor as we love ourselves we are lying! We are being dishonest! We may ignore it and others may be fooled, but we can't pull the wool over the eyes of God! There is no honest relationship with God, Jesus, or the Spirit without love for one another. Yet, we continue to treat "loving our neighbor" as if it were one of the many spiritual options we have to pick up some day. It's not optional!

Love is not love without honesty! "I knew that!"—didn't you?

NOTES
1. Tan, Paul Lee, *Encyclopedia of 7700 Illustrations*, p. 561.
2. Doan, Eleanor, *Speaker's Sourcebook* (Grand Rapids: Zondervan, 1960), pp. 126-127.
3. "Proverbs," *The Expositor's Bible Commentary*, vol. 5), p. 972.
4. Ibid., pp. 975-976.
5. Tan, *Encyclopedia of 7700 Illustrations*, p. 464.
6. "Proverbs," *The Expositor's Bible Commentary*, vol. 5, p. 1077.

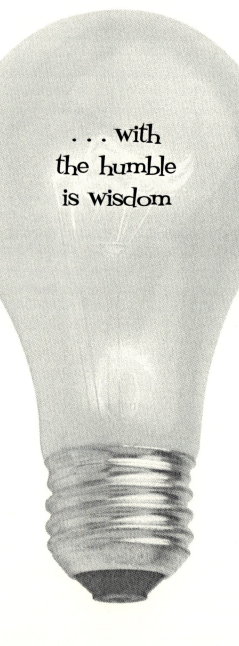

CHAPTER SEVEN
"Don't Get Mad - Get Even!"

My favorite kind of story line is someone standing against impossible odds. In the movies it's *300 Spartans, Star Wars, Zulu, The Magnificent Seven, Gettysburg, Saving Private Ryan,* and *Gods and Generals.* I love historical events that involved uncommon valor. Like Custer's last stand where less than three hundred soldiers tried to fight off three to five thousand Indians; the battle of Roarks Drift where less than two hundred British soldiers withstood some ten hours of attacks from four thousand Zulu warriors; and of course, the valiant men of the Alamo, who held off a giant Mexican Army for thirteen days. These are all thrilling historical moments for those of us who love to study that kind of thing.

Every war in every historical period had its stories of amazing courage while facing impossible odds. Some of the best you'll ever read about are found in the Bible. How many times did God's people find themselves on the short side of the numbers game? Through cunning strategy, incredible bravery, and God's help, the outnumbered people of God won battle after battle. There are incredible stories about Abraham, Joshua, and David winning battles when their enemies vastly outnumbered them.

Standing against impossible odds is a major theme of the Book of Judges. Shamgar, using only an oxgoad, killed six hundred Philistines (3:31). With their smaller army, Deborah and Barak routed the army of Sisera, who had nine hundred iron chariots (4:1-24). God purposely had Gideon pare down his army from thirty-two thousand men to three hundred. These three hundred soldiers surrounded and defeated an army that was so big they were described "as numerous as locusts; their camels were without number, as numerous as the sand on the seashore" (7:12). It was an enormous army, but with God's help and some sneaky tactics, they crushed their enemies (7:1-25). And everyone is familiar with the story of Samson. Especially his killing

I Knew That!

one thousand Philistines with the jawbone of a donkey (15:15), and the thousands he killed when he pulled the temple of Dagon down on top of himself (16:18-31). The Old Testament is full of stories like that.

Courage is not something that was limited to the Old Testament. Who could read of John the Baptist and his fearlessness before Herod and not be impressed with his courage? Anytime I start to think that I'm putting up with a lot of stuff to preach the gospel, I just read Paul's résumé of courage in 2 Corinthians 11, and realize that I know almost nothing about hardship and suffering compared to him. And of course the ultimate example of courage is not found in the Old Testament, but rather in the New, with the written record of Jesus' sacrifice for us. I think of His courage every time I sing the great song, "He Could Have Called Ten Thousand Angels." I would have, but then I don't love the world like He did, nor am I as courageous as Jesus.

Second only to Jesus, I believe the greatest example of courage was Peter standing up for Him in the garden. We often use Peter as an example of blundering and being impatient. In fact, because he denied Jesus three times during the mock trials that final night, we even use him to illustrate weakness. Nevertheless, he was probably one of the bravest men in the entire Bible. Who else would have stepped out of the boat and walked on the water to Jesus? The eleven ship-hugging apostles spent the rest of their lives saying, "I should have." I suspect the same faith that caused him to walk on the water later led him to walk to that inverted cross in Rome not too many years later. (Tradition says he was crucified upside-down, at his request, because he felt unworthy to die like Jesus did.)

Still, as mentioned, what really stands out to me as an incredible act of courage on Peter's part was his willingness to fight the crowd that came to arrest Jesus in Gethsemane. This was no small contingent of men who were coming to arrest Jesus. The Bible describes a great multitude of men who were armed and ready for action. The crowd included representatives from the Sanhedrin, who stayed in the background, but were still noticed by Jesus, and a huge contingent of temple officers. Along with them was a cohort of soldiers from the garrison of Roman soldiers stationed just outside the temple area. A cohort, which was one-tenth of a legion, could be as big as 600 men when at full strength, or as small as a detachment of 200 men, which would still have been more than adequate for this particular assignment.[1]

Against this army of armed men Peter drew his sword and attacked. He cut off the right ear of Malchus, a slave of the high priest. Jesus stopped him and healed the wounded man (John 18:8-11), but what an amazing act of courage! Since they only had two swords among them (Luke 22:38), I don't think Peter was depending on the ten other apostles to join in. Did he think that Jesus would call down those legions of angels or was he just willing to die defending his Savior?

Why did Jesus tell him to put his sword away? Was it because He didn't want any of the remaining eleven apostles to be harmed? He'd mentioned that as a prophecy He was interested in fulfilling, which is why He requested from the crowd that they be released. Maybe it was simply a matter of Peter interfering with the plan. Jesus came down from heaven to die for the world and it was time.

Another, or maybe an additional possibility for why Jesus stopped Peter was to stop him before his anger led him to sin. Anger causes people to do illogical things like drawing their swords on several hundred armed soldiers. Not only does anger make us irrational, but also it can make us ungodly. Maybe Jesus didn't want Peter to start down a road that would not only get them all killed, but foster a spirit in him that was unlike Christ.

CONTROLLED OR OUT-OF-CONTROL?

Before we go any further in studying this subject, let's remember two important things. First, we've all slapped our forehead and said, "I knew that" because we got angry and did something we shouldn't have. There have probably been more "I'm sorry" statements made as a result of getting angry than any other of the many reasons for which we might offer an apology. "I'm sorry. I just lost it there for a few minutes," has been said by nearly every person who ever lived. Or we've said, "I didn't mean to say that. I was just angry!" The possibilities are endless. Not only have we "been there—done that," but also we all knew it was wrong before it happened! Classic "I knew that"!

Secondly, we need to concede that not all anger is bad. Paul assumed that when he said in Ephesians 4:26, "BE ANGRY, AND yet DO NOT SIN." The sin may not be the anger but what we do with it. If we care about something we will respond emotionally to things that negatively impact what we care about. Anger is really just negative passionate feelings. When kept in check, it is not automatically wrong. Keeping it in check is the hard part. That is why Paul added the double encouragement, "do not let the sun go down on your anger," then in the next verse, "and do not give the devil an opportunity" (v. 27).

Controlled anger must be temporary. Sunset is not a legalistic limit. The idea of dumping anger out of our systems as soon as we can is sound advice. Anger that festers and is allowed to grow nearly always turns into some sin that Satan can exploit and enlarge. That is why it's not just a matter of controlling our anger, but of getting rid of it. As we all know, that is easier said

I Knew That!

than done, but it can be done.

Another instance when anger does not have to be bad is when we get angry over sin. Again, this is tricky territory. The line between righteous indignation and self-righteousness is a very thin line. We should get angry anytime Satan wins, but if we become un-Christlike in our reaction to sin, we've given him an even greater victory. There is a place, however, for gut-level anger over our personal sin and using that to motivate us to live more consistent and holy lives. I've known many people who couldn't give up bad habits until they simply got angry with themselves and made it happen.

With all that being said, we must understand that anger rarely produces anything good. It is a life-long struggle for every one of us. Depending on our personalities, we may live in a world of perpetual turmoil because of the amount of anger in our lives. Some people are so tense, stressed out, and anxious that their entire day is spent going from one explosion of anger to another. We excuse them by saying that they just have "a short fuse" or "an explosive personality," but it's really just poor self-control, and it's more Satan-like than Christlike.

The world says, "Don't get mad—get even." You've probably seen that on a bumper sticker or T-shirt. The idea, I assume, is to channel one's anger into revenge and let the satisfaction of "pay back" make you feel a lot better. If ever there was a bumper sticker from hell, it's that one. Satan takes a truthful statement, like "Don't get mad," and simply adds just a little something to it to change it. Kind of like he did in the garden with Eve when he only added one little word to God's command. God told Adam and Eve that if they ate from the forbidden tree they would surely die, but Satan told Eve, "You surely will not die" (Genesis 3:4). As the old country preacher said, "There was a little *not* in the Devil's tale." It was just a little change, but it changed everything.

Jesus warned against getting angry and basically said, "Don't let it happen." In the Sermon on the Mount, He compared being angry with a brother to committing murder. He wasn't talking about the impact on the recipient of the anger. Obviously, we'd rather someone be angry with us than murder us. He was describing how God would view the heart of the one who was full of anger. It's not the kind of heart that is pleasing to God. He wants our hearts to be filled with love, and that means there is no place for anger in our hearts if we want to have a relationship with Him (Matthew 5:21-22).

In the same sermon, Jesus went on to point out that anger towards someone has a direct impact on our spiritual relationship with God. He said,

Therefore if you are presenting your offering at the altar, and there remember that your brother has something against you, leave your offering there before the altar and go; first be reconciled to your brother, and then come and present your offering.
—vv. 23-24

There were few things as important to the Jewish people as their offering to God, but Jesus said that it was a waste of time if they were angry or in a strained relationship with their brother. The sacrifice that we offer is not an animal, but our bodies offered as living sacrifices to God (Romans 12:1). How much more important is it for us when everything we do is worship to God?

We can't harbor anger in our hearts and go on with our relationship with God as if nothing were wrong. Anger doesn't bring us closer to God, but rather becomes a tool that Satan can use to destroy our relationship with Him. Everyone gets angry now and then. When that happens, God wants us to seek reconciliation while Satan wants us to seek revenge. To whom are we going to listen?

Solomon said, "Do not say, 'I will repay evil'; Wait for the LORD, and He will save you" (Proverbs 20:22). The spirit of revenge or "pay-back" has always been a spirit that is ungodly. It's a cancer that eats away the spirit of God in our lives and puts us under the control of Satan. The sooner we can submit to God's will and turn the judging over to Him, the healthier we will be—both emotionally and spiritually. With few (if any) exceptions, when we allow ourselves to be led by anger, we are not being led by Jesus.

Even in the secular world anger is rarely productive and flattering. Some notable quotes bear this out. I particularly like the ones that have a play-on-words.

"The prudent man does not let his temper boil over lest he get into hot water."
"Anger is just one letter short of danger!"
"Anger is a wind which blows out the lamp of the mind."
The wit and wisdom of Benjamin Franklin gave us "Anger is never without a reason, but seldom with a good one." And the well-known humorist, Will Rogers said, "People who fly into a rage always make a bad landing."[2]
Some of the best quotes about anger, especially in explaining why we should avoid it, come from someone who was around two to three millennia before Will or Benjamin, and he got his material from God.

I Knew That!

SOLOMON SAYS—ANGER LEADS TO SIN!

If a person is practicing right, there should be no difference in basketball between a practice session and a game. We all know, of course, that there is a big difference. It's not so much the desire to win, because you always want to win—even in practice. The big difference is primarily the presence of an audience. The presence of spectators changes it from a game to a performance. It's why the adrenaline rush is so high and why some basketball players never quite play as well in a game as they do in practice. I've known many good basketball players who did well in practice, but when they got into a game, with an audience watching and screaming support, their eyes glazed over and their fingers became all thumbs.

The presence of spectators also causes some players to develop an acute case of "grand-standing." Some would "grand-stand" by making fancy passes and taking shots they'd never take in practice. All to gain the admiration of the spectators. Often, however, it only got them a scowl from the coach and a spot on the bench to keep warm.

I still remember, mostly from junior high days, how we thought that "losing it" or "getting mad" on the court was "so cool." We somehow thought it made everyone sit in awe of us, wondering what we were going to do now that we were "ticked off." We'd sling elbows, plow into set screens, and have stare-downs with any opponent who thought he could push us around. Getting mad was an attention getter! While we may have gotten a little more attention from the crowd, all it got us on the court was fouls, missed baskets, and lost games. The coach wasn't impressed, the referee wasn't impressed, and the only ones in the audience who liked it were the ones too immature to understand how unproductive it was. Bottom line: Being a hothead didn't make us look cool, it just made us look foolish.

I've played basketball for over forty years and I still don't understand why people waste time getting angry at the referee. I've never seen one change his mind because of being yelled at and abused, yet people who are supposedly mature adults continue to act like fools at every basketball game by screaming and ranting at the ref. It's one thing to be an inexperienced grand-standing junior high school hothead, but it's a lot worse to be an adult who is out of control with anger over a ball game.

Solomon said,

Don't Get Mad - Get Even!

A wise man is cautious and turns away from evil,
But a fool is arrogant and careless.
A quick-tempered man acts foolishly,
And a man of evil devices is hated.
—Proverbs 14:16-17

Remember one of the reasons Paul told us to remove anger as soon as possible was to keep from giving Satan an opportunity to use it for sin (Ephesians 4:27). Anger leads to sin if it isn't kept in check. It makes us say things we shouldn't. It drives us to retaliate, to strike back, and to hurt in ways we'd never dream of under normal circumstances. Even if we truly don't want to be seen by others as foolish, anger labels us for the world to see.

Who are the people who get the most offensive and outrageous at sports events? It's not only the drunks and malcontents. It's the normally respectable parents, workers, citizens, and neighbors, who just "lose it" and are often embarrassed about it later. Who are the folks who have all the law enforcement people worried about "road rage"? Again, it's not just crooks, bikers, drunkards, and maniacs. It's average people who are aggressive drivers and can't stand it when things don't go their way in traffic.

James warned us about what anger could lead to when he wrote,

This you know, my beloved brethren. But everyone must be quick to hear, slow to speak and slow to anger; for the anger of man does not achieve the righteousness of God.
—James 1:19-20

He seems to be telling us to do those things that will keep us from getting angry. Anger does nothing for bringing us closer to God. In fact, the opposite is usually true. Anger leads us to ungodly thoughts and actions. Anger is an open invitation to Satan to take control of our lives and turn us into the fools that Solomon talked about.

It should scare us to realize how vulnerable we become when we get angry. It's the source of apologies, regrets, broken relationships, and shipwrecked faith. We need to mourn the death of wisdom and grieve over the loss of godliness that anger brings to our lives. Maybe then we will keep it in check and not let anger lead us to sin. Let's change that oft seen bumper sticker to "Don't get mad—get grieving!"

I Knew That!

SOLOMON SAYS—ANGER IS NEGATIVE PASSION!

Someone once said, "Anger is pride on fire." Laying aside for now the complications of pride, it's normal for all of us to have flare-ups of anger. Anger is like a small blaze in the heart that burns the conscience as it boils the blood. Anger is a fact of life, and like fire, it must not be played with or left unattended. It can be controlled and used for good, or it can build, spread, and destroy in unimaginable ways. If it is not extinguished entirely, it can smolder with a slow burn, then build to a raging blaze, and consume home, happiness, and the hope of heaven.

What is the difference between the flare-up of anger and the consuming burn of vengeance? Time and damage! The more time, the more the damage! Anger and vengeance are both negative passions, which is simply a nice way of describing hatred. "Wait a second," someone screams, "I can get angry without it involving hatred!" Only if you stop it quickly enough! Why do you think it's such a spiritually dangerous thing for us to get angry? Anger is negative passion that flares up and is brought under control, or it turns into bitterness, strife, and a spirit of revenge or retaliation—i.e., hatred! What are the other alternatives?

That is why Jesus warned us not to be angry with our brothers (Matthew 5:21-22), why Paul told us not to let it lead us to sin (Ephesians 4:26-27), and why he warned us "never take your own revenge, beloved, but leave room for the wrath of God, for it is written, 'VENGEANCE IS MINE, I WILL REPAY, says the Lord.'" (Romans 12:19).

The Apostle John told us that if we hate our brother we are in darkness, which is the opposite of walking in the light and being covered by the blood of Jesus (1 John 1:7; 2:9,11). He went on to point out that "Everyone who hates his brother is a murderer; and you know that no murderer has eternal life abiding in him" (1 John 3:15). This is very serious stuff when you realize that anger is a sudden burst of hatred! No wonder we need to get rid of it before the sun sets!

Solomon declared, "Hatred stirs up strife, But love covers all transgressions" (Proverbs 10:12). Strife is an old-fashioned word for division and fighting. Hatred stirs it up! How do people usually respond to anger? With anger! Angry people do not build relationships, lighten the heart, or raise the level of joy in any setting. They don't lengthen life or improve the quality of it. They are carriers of strife, misery, and maliciousness. The only transgressions anger covers is dwarfing them with bigger ones. It should frighten us to the bone to realize that love is the antithesis of hatred and anger.

I really like Solomon's advice in Proverbs 15:17-18. It truly sounds like the voice of experience. He said,

> *Better is a dish of vegetables where love is,*
> *Than a fattened ox served with hatred.*
> *A hot-tempered man stirs up strife,*
> *But the slow to anger calms a dispute.*

I am not exactly known as a connoisseur of vegetables. In fact, I have often reflected to others that if God had intended on us living on green stuff, He'd have given us hide, horns, and utters. I eat green beans, corn, carrots, and broccoli (if it's covered in cheese sauce), but I don't "love 'em." I can't image going out to dinner at a nice restaurant and purposely choosing only green stuff. My wife does that all the time. For me—give me meat! Preferably a huge medium-rare prime rib and a butter soaked baked potato (see—I like veggies).

Solomon says, It's better to graze in a vegetable garden than eat a T-bone steak if the atmosphere is one of love. After all, who wants to eat a nice steak that is served with hatred? Have you ever tried to enjoy a nice meal when the air was so thick with strife that you could cut it with your unused steak knife? It's not fun. Anger robs everything and everybody of joy, peace, and love. The only thing it gives is indigestion.

SOLOMON SAYS—ANGER TESTS OUR SELF-CONTROL!

Anger is not a "use it or lose it" commodity. It's more a "lose it, don't use it" challenge. We all "get mad" occasionally. So we get mad—now what! Now the challenge begins. Are we going to control it or turn it loose? Retaliate? Strike out verbally or even physically? Satan whispers in our ear, "Do it!" Our ego screams, "Do it!" Every fiber of our adrenaline-intoxicated body shouts, "Do it!" We may even have friends/peers cheering, "Do it!" But—down in our hearts—in the deep recesses of our souls—we hear the soft voice of Jesus saying, "Wait—let it pass!"

Did you ever notice how totally anti-anger the fruit of the Spirit is? Love, joy, and peace are all attitudes that clearly are the antithesis of anger. In fact, they destroy anger—or are destroyed by anger. Patience, kindness, goodness, faithfulness, gentleness, and self-control are all ways that we deal with anger. Goodness, faithfulness, and self-control are the attitudes and qualities we develop in our hearts, while patience, kindness, and gentleness describe the way we respond to those who make us angry (Galatians 5:22-23).

Everything about the fruit of the Spirit makes it clear that we must be proactive in dealing with anger in our lives. Anger is an enemy of the Spirit.

Remembering that anger is simply negative passion, listen to what Paul says immediately after listing the fruit of the Spirit. "Now those who belong to Christ Jesus have crucified the flesh with its passions and desires" (v. 24). Since we belong to Jesus, that means we are controlled by Jesus and not by our passions, especially negative passions. Part of crucifying the flesh must certainly include nailing anger to the cross! Living for Jesus means we must be consistently Christlike. As Paul says, "If we live by the Spirit, let us also walk by the Spirit" (v. 25). And just in case we don't understand what that means, Paul gives a clear application of what it means to walk by the Spirit in the next verse. "Let us not become boastful, challenging one another, envying one another" (v. 26). He added to that by encouraging us to "restore" a brother who sins, in a "spirit of gentleness" (6:1).

Isn't it interesting that Paul immediately applies walking by the Spirit to boasting, challenging, and envying one another? He's talking about more than petty selfishness and competition. He's talking about "passions and desires" that should be "crucified." These are all things that come from and cause anger! Crucify it!

Anger has never been a flattering quality. Solomon says,

> *Like a city that is broken into and without walls*
> *Is a man who has no control over his spirit.*
> —Proverbs 25:28

> *A fool always loses his temper,*
> *But a wise man holds it back.*
> —Proverbs 29:11

> *A fool's anger is known at once,*
> *But a prudent man conceals dishonor.*
> —Proverbs 12:16

> *He who is slow to anger is better than the mighty,*
> *And he who rules his spirit, than he who captures a city.*
> —Proverbs 16:32

Everyone gets mad—but not everyone controls it! You're thinking, "I knew that!" So why do we have to be reminded of it so often?

SOLOMON SAYS—ANGER DESTROYS COMPASSION!

It must have been utter chaos! Every sick, blind, lame, and withered person in the region wanted to be the first person into the pool at Bethesda after the magical moving of the water. According to legend, that person would be healed of whatever malady he had. It was a small pool, so the crowd must have been frantic in their efforts to be close to the water. There must have been crutches swinging and elbows flying as people pushed and shoved for position. (Kind of like a sale at Target!)

One man, who had been crippled for a long time and was obviously unable to get any closer to the water, simply lay on his pallet with hopelessness written all over his face. Unbeknownst to him, Jesus had been observing him. No softer or more compassionate heart ever beat in the body of a person than the heart of Jesus. He healed him! He told the man to take up his pallet and walk! It was not because of his faith—in fact, it had nothing to do with faith! It had everything to do with compassion! (John 5:2-9).

What a day of rejoicing that must have been! Wrong! If anyone other than the healed man was rejoicing, the Bible doesn't tell us. It does tell us about some religious people who were angry about the whole thing. Some of the Jews who witnessed the miracle—ignored it and only saw a man carrying his pallet on the Sabbath, which according to their traditions was a violation of the Law. They not only didn't see an act of compassion, but also they felt none themselves. They only saw something that made them angry enough to want to hurt Jesus (vv. 10-16). Anger is ugly enough on its own, but it really turns monstrous when combined with self-righteousness.

You know from experience that anger drives compassion right out of your heart. That's why people can do things when they are angry that they could never do when they are calm, cool, and collected. We may call it "a fit of passion," "temporary insanity," or even an "extenuating circumstance," but it's still just anger. Because of anger, a heart that is normally soft and sensitive can be hardened to the point of losing all sympathy, sorrow, regrets, and compassion for others. As we have already seen, it drives the fruit of the Spirit right out of our hearts.

Listen to what Solomon says about what anger does to us.

He who is slow to anger has great understanding,
But he who is quick-tempered exalts folly.
A tranquil heart is life to the body,
But passion is rottenness to the bones.
—Proverbs 14:29-30

I Knew That!

We are just beginning to understand how damaging stress is to our physical and emotional well-beings. Stress and anger are negative passions that Solomon says bring "rottenness to the bone." Maybe he is talking about a literal deterioration of the physical body, or maybe he is referring to the depth of the negative impact anger has on us. We talk about being "bad to the bone," and that is what anger does for us. Maybe Solomon is talking about both forms of rottenness. Either way, it's not something that brings us closer to being like the compassionate Jesus!

In Proverbs 22:24-25, Solomon warns us about where we learn to be angry people. He said,

> *Do not associate with a man given to anger;*
> *Or go with a hot-tempered man,*
> *Or you will learn his ways*
> *And find a snare for yourself.*

While we all have the capacity to be angry people, anger for the most part is a learned behavior. It is a learned response to things that happen that we don't like. Parents who explode and deal with life's disappointments by getting angry, teach their children that anger is an appropriate way to respond. Or, if parents allow their children to get away with responding to things with anger, they learn that it works and is a viable way to get what you want. Anger is a poor coping skill that we allow our children to learn and develop. They can say what they want about how quiet and mild-mannered a young boy was, who all of a sudden took a gun to school and shot people; but you can be fully assured, that was not the first time he responded to things with violent anger.

From others' examples or from lack of discipline, we learn the way of anger and "find a snare for" ourselves—and unfortunately, those around us.

The sad truth is that many thrive on anger. We all want to feel passion about something. If we can't find the right things or people to feel passionate about, we will find negative things to feel passionate about. Anger is a passion. It makes people feel fully alive to have something that drives them, pumps the adrenaline, and gives them focus. Sometimes it's hate, racism, and bigotry, and sometimes it's just a negative, cynical, and self-righteous attitude.

I have noticed throughout the years that some Christians seem to stay angry all the time. They have that church-chip on their shoulder and they are always looking for someone to knock it off. It used to trouble me greatly. I used to wonder, "Why do some people just look for something to be upset about?" Some folks are always in a turmoil about something they don't like, or agree with, or "have doctrinal concerns" with. Every church has some members like that. They corner elders in the foyer and chew their ears off; they write notes and letters of "concern" to the church giving ultimatums and making threats; and they know exactly what God meant to put in all those "where the Bible is silent" areas of the New Testament.

It finally dawned on me one day that being angry about something is what gave them their passion in their religion. They only felt really alive and "faithful" when they were angry about something! I can understand that—but what does that do to their heart of compassion? Satan loves it when we fill our hearts with negative passion rather than Christlike passion.

That is why Solomon warned,

Do not rejoice when your enemy falls,
And do not let your heart be glad when he stumbles;
Or the LORD will see it and be displeased,
And turn His anger away from him.
                                            –Proverbs 24:17-18

Wow! Not only does our anger towards someone damage our hearts and make God unhappy with us, but it causes God to start feeling sorry for our enemy! What God wants us to do is,

If your enemy is hungry, give him food to eat;
And if he is thirsty, give him water to drink;
For you will heap burning coals on his head,
And the LORD will reward you.
                                            –Proverbs 25:21-22

We need to change our worldview of anger. Instead of "Don't get mad—get even," we can change it to "Don't get mad—get even—with Satan!" Show compassion instead of anger and *drive him nuts*!

The choice is ours. Like Solomon said,

A gentle answer turns away wrath,
But a harsh word stirs up anger.
                                            –Proverbs 15:1

I Knew That!

HOLY ANGER?

Was Jesus angry when He cleansed the temple? It seems to me that He was angry about the abuses taking place in His Father's house. You'd at least have to call it righteous indignation. He was passionate about how the temple should be used. We must remember, however, that He never let it lead Him to sin, He never lost control, and He, unlike us, couldn't possibly be misjudging the hearts of the people He drove out of the temple that day.

There is a place for holy anger. We need to hate sin and be angry about Satan trying to pull us into it. That's why we must "fight the good fight," "resist Satan," and make him flee. This holy anger or righteous indignation must have three things. (These will preach.)

It must be controlled.
It must be constructive.
It must be Christlike.

If it meets all three of these requirements, then it may be all right to be angry, but I must warn you, very few people have ever been able to pull it off. In fact—maybe only One truly has.

One of the many stories from the travels of Sinbad comes from the time he and his sailors landed on a tropical island to search for provisions. They saw in the tops of tall trees some coconuts, which would be perfect for quenching their thirst and satisfying their hunger. There was a problem. They couldn't get to them. None of the men knew how to climb the trees and they had no way of reaching the coconuts. Their solution came from the monkeys who were already in the trees watching the helpless men and chattering their disapproval at them. Sinbad and his men began to throw sticks and stones at the monkeys. Rather than scare them away, it enraged them. In retaliation, the monkeys grabbed the coconuts and began throwing them at the men on the ground. Before long, the sailors had all the coconuts they could carry. The angry monkeys had played right into the hands of the men and became food gatherers for them.[3]

Paul warned us about the "flaming arrows of the evil one" that we need to defend against (Ephesians 6:16). Maybe we need to think of Satan throwing sticks and stones at us, and waiting for us to get angry and play right into his hands. What God intended to be higher ground for His followers can also be a good place from which to throw coconuts. That is, if we are more interested in monkeying around than we are about living for Jesus. (Sorry, but our anger does make us look more like them than Him.)

Don't Get Mad - Get Even!

Lord, help me not to be angry—ever. If I do, may it be short lived and may I not sin when it happens. Help me to remember these things before I do them rather than slap my head afterwards and say, "I knew that!"

NOTES
1. Harrison, Everett F., *A Short Life of Christ*, (Grand Rapids: Eerdmans, 1968), p. 199.
2. Doan, Eleanor, *Speaker's Scourcebook*, pp. 21-22.
3. Tan, Paul Lee, *Encyclopedia of 7700 Illustrations*, pp. 130-131.

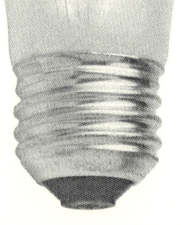

CHAPTER EIGHT
"Friends Are Friends Forever"

My theology of weddings is as liberal as the day is long. Of course I'm not really talking about theology since the Bible has "zilch" to say about weddings, but I am saying that I'm a bride's best friend when it comes to doing whatever she wants done. I'm as open as the Bible is when it comes to what can be done at a wedding. In spite of the fact that Roman Catholicism made marriage a church sacrament many centuries ago, it is and always will be primarily a fulfillment of the law of the land.

Having said that, I must point out that most of the hundreds of weddings over which I have officiated (that sounds like I was a referee rather than a "licensed and ordained man of the cloth"—whatever that means) were very traditional events. In fact, they were nearly all so traditional that they all looked alike. The weddings that stand out in my memory bank are the ones where someone fainted or dropped a ring.

I have seen the full array of music used at weddings, too. There have been singers of all kinds and numbers, there were many that simply had the traditional organ or piano music, and a few even had a string quartet. I do remember the one that had an accordion player who played from the back of the church building. Oddly enough, he played only traditional wedding music and it sounded just like an organ. It just made me a little uncomfortable seeing him standing back there during the ceremony. I kept visualizing him breaking into "Beer Barrel Polka" at any moment.

One of the first weddings that I ever performed where they played contemporary music was a very moving and emotional wedding. I especially remember that while the just-pronounced "husband and wife" lit the Unity Candle, the soundman played a recording of "Friends Are Friends Forever" and it had everyone in tears. We all knew that they were best of friends and that would give them an incredible jump on building their marriage relation-

I Knew That!

ship. It was, and still is, a very popular song of closeness, commitment, and loyalty. Real genuine friends have a bond that can last a lifetime.

Of course it doesn't always turn out that way. Friends are not always friends forever. As we grow and change, our interests and priorities change. Unfortunately, people don't change the same way at the same time. What once was an incredible bond can fall apart as the glue that held it together changes. That is why we don't have the same friends in elementary school as we do in high school, and those same friends that we thought would be friends forever—just aren't anymore. We changed tremendously through the years and we moved on to new relationships.

I taught Bible Class at a Christian school for seven years. I had the senior class most of those years. I told each class that in spite of how close they were and how much they felt eternally bound together, very few high school friendships last past graduation. There are always exceptions, but for the most part, the friends they would make in college would come much nearer being lifelong friends than the people they were close to in high school. They never believed me, and they always knew that they would be the exception, but they weren't. Many times, even students who went off to the same college found new friends and eventually stopped hanging around together.

That's natural and to be expected. Even those of us who have been around long enough to be well past young adulthood remember friends that we had back in those young adult years that we're just not close to anymore. We're different people than we were back then.

Sometimes we just grow apart, and sometimes we rip apart. If someone proves not to be trustworthy and not the friend we thought they were, it can destroy the friendship and be one of the most painful experiences of our lives. That's a risk we take every time we make a new friend, but in the grand scheme of things—it's a risk worth taking.

A BLESSING—A NEED—A MYSTERY?

Friends are one of life's greatest blessings. Profound? Hardly. That is probably one of the easiest statements about which each of us can say, "I knew that." Yet, as fitting as the whole thesis of this book is, it's one of the most oft-forgotten principles of life. We focus so much time and energy on success, gaining wealth, and accumulating things; yet we all know that the greatest joys we experience in life come from relationships. When was the last time you attended a funeral where the eulogy centered on the deceased person's wealth, position, and possessions? The only thing that mattered was the relationships the person had, why they were loved, and why they will be missed.

Hopefully, there was a relationship with God, which changed the entire perspective people had about their loss.

Having friends could be described as the most important thing we do in life, especially when we consider that Jesus must be at the top of the list. We need friends. We have been created by God as social beings. Friends give life meaning. They give us our sense of belonging and acceptance, which in turn contribute to our self-esteem and emotional health. Because of friends we learn to love, respect, give, and share. Our best memories come from experiences we've had with people we love. They make us better people and greatly improve the quality (and quantity) of our lives.

Isn't it odd that such an important thing as having and keeping friends is virtually left up to chance? When and where do we learn about how to have friends? There is no training or schooling in the art of making friends. We grow up learning by observation and basically relying on trial and error. Is it any wonder that so many people don't know how to make and keep friends? We rely on "hitting if off" or having "the right chemistry" to get our friends. If we later discover that "the chemistry's just not right" we dissolve the relationship and move on to another one. It shouldn't be a surprise that many people approach marriage the same way.

All relationships, if they are important to us, must be built not just left up to chance. This is true whether the relationship involves friends, marriage, or our walk with God. Good growing relationships must be worked on, cultivated, and improved. This takes devotion and commitment. This means that we must want that relationship and put forth effort to make it work.

In Alan McGinnis's classic book *The Friendship Factor*, he stated that "rule number one for deepening your friendships is: *assign top priority to your relationships.*"[1] Don't rely on "hitting it off" or "chemistry" but rather invest yourself in people and build relationships that will bless you and them.

I have observed that for a lot of people, friendships become a lower priority as they get older. As we spend several years investing ourselves in our families and careers, we suddenly realize that we don't have any really close friends. Oh, there are the good folks that we go out to eat with after church Sunday night or the neighbors we grill-out with occasionally, but close friends? We don't have time for that! So we don't have someone with whom to share our joys and sorrows. We don't have someone we can call at 2:00 A.M.. and ask for help. We also, don't have someone who will pull us out of our castle and comfort zone to help them. After all, family and job are higher priorities and they are all we really need.

I wouldn't take issue with those priorities, but I would take issue with the thinking that family and job are "all we really need." We need friends, and while our spouses may be our very best friends, we need other friends who love us, help us, and need us. We need the encouragement and support of friends. We need others with whom we can share our life's experiences. We need friends who understand us, who will listen to us, and who will trust us to do the same for them. We need friends who will hold us accountable for our inconsistencies, weaknesses, and bad choices. We need others who will accept us, include us, and appreciate us.

We need as much experience in relationship building as we can get. After all, what is this whole business of "being a Christian" all about, if it's not building a relationship with Christ and God? If we can't build relationships with our spouses and friends, whom we see, how can we build a relationship with God whom we have not seen? That's the same question John tosses out to us regarding loving one another. In 1 John 4:20, John points out that loving God is totally dependent on loving our brothers. If we think that they are two completely different things and believe we can say we love Him while hating our brother, we are liars. The way we show our love for God is by loving others. Anything else is just talk or theory.

How do we give, sacrifice, and share for God without doing those things for others? We need relationships that teach us how to be unselfish, where we learn what commitment really is, and how vital and central communication is to every relationship. What makes us think that we can build a successful relationship with God when we haven't learned how to build ones with friends? Sometimes a poor relationship with God is simply indicative of the quality of relationships we have on earth.

I concur with Ralph Waldo Emerson when he said, "God evidently does not intend us all to be rich, or powerful or great, but he does intend us all to be friends."[2] I don't think aging, marriage, or careers change that. Emerson was not just voicing a jewel of wisdom, but stating a biblical truth. God wants us to have friends. Friendship is a blessing from God that we all need; yet for some mysterious reason, we tend to forget how important it is.

A FRIEND IS A FRIEND IS A FRIEND!

Have you ever tried to define friendship? It's not easy. It almost fits into one of those categories like "I can't explain it, but I know it when I see it." It happens! It clicks! It's fun! We know that it includes some deep philosophical "stuff," but mostly we just know that it feels good to have friends—to be wanted and needed—and missed.

Emerson said, "A friend is someone who will make us do what we can when we are saying we can't."[3] I like that, even though it applies to moms, dads, teachers, and angry football coaches. The truth is, many of us are what we are today because of a friend who cheered, "You can do it!"

At the time of this writing, it's been thirty-five years since I preached my first full-length Sunday morning sermon. The poor folks in the little country church in Morvan, Georgia, had to endure my first pulpit odyssey and yet they still insisted on paying me twenty dollars. Aside from the little boy who stood and vomited in the aisle during my sermon, it went rather well and started me on the road to giving my life to the ministry of the Word.

It never would have happened if my buddy Bill hadn't encouraged me to do it. He lined up the speaking appointment, gave me the material with which to prepare the sermon, and told me over and over how God gave me the talent to do a good job. That same sermon was preached in churches all over south Georgia from 1968 through 1970. I can still remember it today—and I wouldn't preach it if my life depended on it. Still, I am a preacher today because of the grace of God, a lot of good teachers and forgiving brothers, and one special friend who said, "You can do it!"

I like the words of a not-so-well-known poem entitled "Friends." Like many great poems, the author is unknown.

> *The joy of being friends is just*
> *A simple code of faith and trust,*
> *A homey comradeship that stays*
> *The threatened fear of darker days;*
> *The kind of faith that brings to light*
> *The good, the beautiful, and bright;*
> *And best and blest, and true and rare—*
> *Is having friends who love and care!*[4]

Friends may not be friends forever because not all friends stay friends. Yet, the real beauty of friendship is that you can always develop new ones. I have had good friends all my life. Some have lasted for decades and some for just months as job transfers put thousands of miles in the way of building deeper relationships, or other interests just caused us to drift apart. I have loads of great memories of friends. And I have a minute number of painful ones, too. Along the way there were friends who disappointed me or broke a trust, but praise God—they are the exception and not the rule. Right now, I'm blessed with some of the best friends I've ever had.

I Knew That!

Maybe that's why I am drawn to Bible stories like David and Jonathan, Ruth and Naomi, Paul and Barnabus, Jesus and John, and most of all, Jesus and me. Isn't it wonderful to know that all the men and women of the Bible had friends? They enjoyed all the blessings of friendship and had a memory-bank full of treasured experiences—just like we do! And the best thing of all is knowing that Jesus wants to be our friend. He's our Lord and Savior first, of course, but He desires a relationship that includes being friends. As we draw closer to Him and begin to be truly like Him, isn't it appropriate to think of Him as our pal, our buddy, our best friend on and off earth? He said that He laid down His life for His friends. Doesn't that include us? He said that His friends are those who do what He commands. Doesn't that describe us? He said, "No longer do I call you slaves; for the slave does not know what his master is doing; but I have called you friends, for all things that I have heard from My Father I have made known to you" (John 15:13-15). Isn't He talking to us? There is no better friend than Jesus.

FRIENDS ARE GIFTS FROM GOD! I KNEW THAT!

I recently finished teaching a class on building intimacy in marriage. In this class we studied a book of the Bible that most of us have avoided like the plague—The Song of Solomon. Once we worked through our cultural hang-ups and remembered that sexual intimacy is a gift from God, it became a rather interesting study. It did strike me as ironic to be reading the advice of Solomon concerning intimacy in marriage when monogamy and biblical oneness seemed to have never crossed his mind. How on earth did he even remember the names of one thousand women, let alone develop an intimate relationship with each one?

As I look at his Proverbs concerning friends, I find myself asking the question, "What kind of friends did he have?" He was the richest and most powerful man in the ancient world, and he, by his own admission, withheld nothing from himself (Ecclesiastes 2:10). And you have to ask yourself how a guy, who had been given wisdom from God early in his life, could do so many utterly selfish things. Isn't wisdom superior to "trial and error," which seems to be his theme in Ecclesiastes? He had to be the ultimate "I knew that" guy! What kind of friends did someone who was given to excess and debauchery attract? How deep could the relationship be? How much could he trust someone not to stick a knife in his back or slip some poison into his food or drink?

At the very least, he should know individuals not to have as a friends. He learned the hard way that "Wealth adds many friends, but a poor man is separated from his friend" (Proverbs 19:4). Just as the Prodigal son of Luke 15 had plenty of friends as long as he had plenty of cash, Solomon must have had lots of "friends" who were willing to help him distribute his wealth. He should have known the value of a friend who loves you for who you are not what you can buy him.

In ancient days the words neighbor and friend were virtually interchangeable in usage and this is reflected in the Bible. Depending on the translation you read, you may have either word used in many passages about close relationships. In Proverbs 12:26, the NIV says, "A righteous man is cautious in friendship, but the way of the wicked leads them astray." The NASB says, "The righteous is a guide to his neighbor, but the way of the wicked leads them astray." Whether you use the word neighbor or friend, the principle is the same; be careful how you pick those with whom you're going to hang around.

A righteous friend, that is one who cares about doing what is right, will not lead you down the wrong road. You can trust her and depend on her, because she will be interested in helping you to be righteous.

One of the subjects that I covered as part of my senior Bible Class was building relationships. I literally taught twelfth graders how to make and keep friends. Even at that age they thought it "just happened." Each year I always had a chalkboard brainstorming session where I wrote down all the things they mentioned about what they wanted in a friend. Every time I did this, the same qualities rose to the top. They were trust, loyalty, and understanding. These are things that we all want in a friend and if they are missing or prove to be violated, the relationship can be seriously, and ever permanently, damaged.

Solomon said to pick your friends carefully. A good one will be a guide to better living and a closer walk with God. The wrong kind of friend can get you seriously off track and have painful consequences. As the wise king says in Proverbs 13:20, "He who walks with wise men will be wise, But the companion of fools will suffer harm."

Remember what happened when Pinocchio followed his new "friends" to Pleasure Island? They had a big time breaking windows, smoking cigars, and just being juvenile delinquents. They gradually grew hooves, long ears, and equine muzzles, as they all turned into donkeys (or something closely related). They turned into what they were acting like. Likewise, if you hang around with fools, you'll end up looking just like them. If you want to improve your intelligence (and probably your looks) spend time with the wise.

One of Solomon's best-known proverbs about friends is found in Proverbs 17:17. "A friend loves at all times, And a brother is born for adversity." A real friend would never have let the Prodigal son get so low that he longed for pig food. A real friend is one who cares and helps when things are tough. We're not talking about fair-weather friends, but the ones who endure the storms of life with you so that you will not have to be alone. There is no curfew on their counsel and no time cards on their compassion. They are 24/7 friends who would feel slighted if you didn't call them and let them know you were hurting. That is why they are so precious—so valuable! They don't come in bunches or by the dozen. They are usually two to four special people in our lives who love us in spite of our weaknesses and mistakes. Who hold our hands in the hospital, cry with us at the graveyard, hug us in our repentance, and pray for us all the time.

Friends are a wonderful gift from God, and hopefully—we are that to them. God wants us to have friends, but He wants us to have deep relationships and not just droves of relationships. When it comes to having friends, it's nice to have quantity, but the real goal is quality. Solomon declared, "A man of many friends comes to ruin, But there is a friend who sticks closer than a brother" (18:24). He seems to be saying that it's better to have one really good, faithful friend that to have a multitude of unreliable friends.[5]

The truth is that many of our "friendships" are really very shallow. Many are really acquaintances, not close friends. We think that because we see each other often, share pleasantries, and enjoy being together that we are real friends. We all have loads of people we think of as friends at church, at work, in our neighborhood, and in our communities, but how many of them would you feel comfortable calling at 3:00 AM. to tell them you need their help? Who would you want calling you at 3:00 AM. and asking you for help? The friend who sticks closer than a brother is the one you can count on, and that's a treasure trully for whom to thank God. Have you? (Smack—Oh yeah, I knew that!)

Speaking of 3:00 AM. calls, I wonder if Solomon ever needed someone to talk to in the middle of the night—someone besides one of his wives or concubines. He clearly had been the recipient of good advice from a friend at some point in his life. Look at Proverbs 27:9: "Oil and perfume make the heart glad, So a man's counsel is sweet to his friend."

Do you have any idea how much of your real-life education came from friends? Think about it! How many of life's important lessons and insights came to you from a wiser, or more experienced friend? Just think of all the pain and embarrassment friends have spared you through the years. Granted, there were times when their "wisdom" was skewed a bit or even wrong, but our lives have been greatly impacted by the advice of friends. From the "birds and the bees" to the "bulls and the bears," we have been educated, enlightened, and "saved" by friends more times than we can even remember.

Friends Are Friends Forever

I can't imagine not having a good friend to go to and ask advice. Every major decision that I have ever made in my life had the input of friends on it somewhere. Most of the time they were simply sounding boards to listen to my options and nod agreement with my conclusions. Other times, they opened my eyes to some things I'd missed and saved me from making some critical mistakes. Then there were the times they gave me the verbal "slap across the face" that I needed, and brought to my attention some inconsistency or stupidity in my life.

Solomon must have had experiences that "slap across the face," too. He wrote, "Faithful are the wounds of a friend, But deceitful are the kisses of an enemy" (Proverbs 27:6). The best friend in the whole world is the one who loves you enough to tell you what you need to hear and not just what you want to hear. It can be very painful, but if it's a "love-lick" from a friend, praise God for such a friend.

When Naaman was told to "Go and wash in the Jordan seven times, and your flesh shall be restored to you and you shall be clean," he not only thought it was a dumb way to cure leprosy, but an insult to his position. In a rage he condemned the whole idea and headed for home. He was stopped by one of his servants, and because of the way that servant spoke to him, I suspect they were pretty good friends and not just slave—master. He told him, ". . . had the prophet told you to do some great thing, would you not have done it? How much more then, when he says to you, 'Wash, and be clean'?" That advice made him stop and think a minute. It was a major "I knew that" moment for him. He ended up turning around and doing what the prophet said and "his flesh was restored like the flesh of a little child" (2 Kings 5:1-14). Don't you know that he was thankful for that counsel the rest of his life?

My abridged version of Solomon's proverb is "Be thankful for friends who love you enough to wound you, because kisses are not always a sign of love." We'd all rather have a kiss than a wound, but the friend who can't give us what's best for us is not really a friend. At the risk of sounding trite, we must remember that sometimes love must be tough. After all, since "God is opposed to the proud, but gives grace to the humble," who's doing you a favor when he just builds your ego? We need friends who have the guts to tell us when we are being jerks or when we have a piece of broccoli stuck between our teeth.

"TO THE BITTER END"

The buzzards break into a beautiful four-part barbershop harmony and sing, "We're your friends! We're your friends! We're your friends to the bitter end." Thus begins one of my favorite songs from any Disney musical animation movie. It's from *The Jungle Book*. Aside from being a wonderful piece of music, it's hysterical to see four buzzards dancing around singing about their loyalty and friendship to a little boy who, in the real world, would have been their dinner.

Most of the Proverbs we've looked at have emphasized how wonderful it is to have good friends. Before we finish up this study, we need to be reminded of the responsibility we have to be good friends to our good friends. This is where you slap your forehead and say, "I knew that!" We all do, but for some reason we have to be reminded over and over.

Friendship is a shared relationship where each fulfills his or her responsibility to contribute and build the relationship. It is a matter of mutual need! As Solomon put it, "Iron sharpens iron, so one man sharpens another" (Proverbs 27:17). When both of us do our jobs and we both benefit from the experience. Our lives are enriched—we are better people! We have given as well as received!

A friendship is only as strong as the commitment each person has to the relationship. When you start thinking of each other as dependable, trustworthy, and loyal, then you have a close relationship (or a Boy Scout troop). This is where we *must remember that friendship is a two-way street*! We must be just as dependable, trustworthy, and loyal to our friends as we expect them to be to us. As Solomon declared, "Do not forsake your own friend or your father's friend. . . ." (Proverbs 27:10). When they have a problem or a need, *be there* for them! That is what separates the real friends from the fair-weather friends. Notice that I said, "*be there*" and not "fix it" or "solve the problem" or "make everything okay." The first and foremost responsibility is "presence." Good friends simply need to be together when times are tough. You probably won't be able to say or do anything to make things "okay," but you can be there to share, comfort, and encourage.

We need to remember that the only time recorded in Scripture where Jesus wept openly was prior to raising His good friend Lazarus from the dead. Even then, He wasn't weeping for Lazarus but hurting for Mary, Martha, and the others who were grieving so deeply. In John 11, the Holy Spirit emphatically states that He loved Lazarus (v. 3) and his sisters Mary and Martha (v. 5). He went to Bethany to raise Lazarus, not because He wanted to do any favors for Lazarus, but because He cared so deeply about the pain His living friends were feeling. He was "deeply moved in spirit" and wept unashamedly (vv. 33-38). What most people forget is the real reason He raised Lazarus from the dead. After declaring to His disciples that Lazarus was dead, He states, ". . .

Friends Are Friends Forever

and I am glad for your sakes that I was not there, so that you may believe" (v. 15). He wanted His disciples/friends to grow in faith. This recorded event, while it shows the power of Jesus and proves His Sonship, is also all about friendship and love. Everything Jesus did was for the sake of His friends. Lazarus, Mary, and Martha were His friends (v. 5) and His disciples were His friends (John 15:13-15).

Jesus knows all about friendship. He wants to be our friend. He paid the ultimate price to prove this friendship. As He stated in John 15:13, "Greater love has no one than this, that one lay down his life for his friends." Before you say, "I knew that," do you remember that He wants us to do the same thing for Him? Absolutely! Paul put it this way, ". . . present your bodies a living and holy sacrifice, acceptable to God, which is your spiritual service of worship" (Romans 12:1).

The next time you sing "What a friend we have in Jesus," think of Jesus singing about what a friend He has in you!

NOTES
1. McGinnis, Alan Loy, *The Friendship Factor* (Minneapolis: Augsburg, 1979), p. 22.
2. Doan, *Speaker's Sourcebook,* p. 106.
3. Ibid.
4. Ibid., p. 108.
5. "Proverbs," *The Expositor's Commentary,* vol. 5, p. 1029.

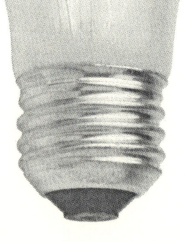

CHAPTER NINE
"Live One Day at a Time"

I never imagined it could happen! It's astounding, mind-boggling, and dramatic. It's one of those life-changing events that so alters your life that you know you will never be the same again! And it happened to me! Unbelievable!

No—I didn't win the Publisher's Clearing House Sweepstakes, and I wasn't kidnapped by aliens (at least I don't remember it). I didn't discover gold, develop cancer, or get invited onto the next *Survivor* show. In fact, I haven't even told my wife about it yet—though I'm sure she suspects something. The members of my congregation are clueless because they think I've always been this way. I'm only in my sixth year of ministry with them, but I'm sure my former two congregations would know that something has happened. It's why I laugh when one of my newer brothers or sisters comments on how "laid back" I am.

Here it is—are you ready? I have learned to actually enjoy having nothing to look forward to! Can you believe it? Maybe you're laughing too hard to see the significance of all this. So before you hurt yourself doubling over, just ask yourself how much of your life is lived anticipating something? How much do you enjoy the thrill of looking forward to something and longing for it to arrive or take place?

I have been an excitement junkie all my life. I've always loved the excitement of planning, anticipating, and imagining what the future will be. I have spent most of my life focusing on the next event. The excitement of anticipation was like electricity to my mind and body. I lived for the next event.

Part of it was simply the enthusiasm of youth that is common to everyone. You know—living for the next birthday, the next Christmas, the next Easter, the next vacation, the next school year, the next accomplishment, license, degree, or whatever. We all experience that. We can't wait for the next year to arrive so we will be "old enough," "legal enough," or "adult enough" to do

I Knew That!

whatever it is we want to do next. Then one day we realize that we've started something that seems to be going faster and faster with each passing year, and we can't figure out how to slow it down.

In my nearly three decades of ministry, I never had a routine or a rut. I lived for the next church event. I thought, I dreamed, and I envisioned new things, all of which provided me with the anticipation/electricity my brain demanded. There were times when the new idea—the new challenge—became more important than the people it was meant to help and the God it was meant to glorify. So I learned my lesson—several times—and started getting excited about what God could do if I'd slow down and let Him be in charge, but I still kept thinking in terms of what He was going to do in the future.

Maybe it's impossible to stop being a Type-A personality, but it sure is possible to change the way you look at life. I know what the Bible says, and I've preached many-a-sermon about the folly of living in the future instead of the present, but it still took nearly half a century for me to learn to simply live for today. To enjoy it, appreciate it, and use it for Him!

Why is it so difficult for us to stop everything and enjoy the here and now? I still love excitement, but I've learned to be excited about the present. I enjoy nature more. I see wild flowers, flittering birds, and ancient trees that I never used to notice. Even with almost thirty years of hunting and fishing behind me, including thousands of hours in tree stands, it has just been recently that I've truly seen the outdoors as God's daily creation. Again, that's probably due to my anticipating a dream buck appearing or a huge fish biting and I rarely noticed the detail that our Father put into this, His canvas, called Earth. And now, days fly by like leaves in the fall and I realize that there aren't too many seasons left. So, with deliberate effort, I try to slow down and enjoy every day.

That may sound like the confessions of a cancer patient, or someone who's recovering from heart surgery, but as far as I know, I'm blessed with great health. Actually, that is part of my motivation. I don't want to wait until I'm counting down my last days or reflecting on near-death surgery before I appreciate every day God gives me. I want to be thankful not maudlin, or guilty, or regretful, or even penitent. I don't want to miss any more of what God does for me because of being too focused on what I hope will happen at some point in the future. "This is the day which the LORD has made; Let us rejoice and be glad in it" (Psalm 118:24).

What about the other side of that coin—the past? Until my children began leaving home and starting families of their own, I never spent much time thinking about the past. Since then, one thing has become very clear—the older you get, the stronger the temptation is to dwell on the past.

Live One Day at a Time

I used not to care much about taking pictures at family events. I didn't even care much about family portraits. It was "living in the past" and why would anyone want to do that when the future looks so exciting? I'm so glad that Mrs. Root didn't agree with my rationale. She took pictures of every birthday, every Christmas, every school program, every Thanksgiving, and—well—everything. Now, as we adjust to being "empty nesters," I wouldn't exchange those pictures for all of Bill Gates' net worth. Like the old hymn we sing, they are "precious memories."

What a blessing it is to have so many precious memories! It's wonderful to reflect and reminisce about the past, but we must not live there. Some folks long for the past with such passion that they can't see anything commendable about the present. To them, the "good old days" were the best days, and the present is simply something to be endured. That robs people of their joy, their sense of gratefulness, and their hope for the future. To look back and rejoice over God's blessings, to learn from our experiences and determine to be good stewards of today, this the way mature Christians use the past, but they don't live in it.

ONE DAY AT A TIME, SWEET JESUS!

How many clichés have you heard through the years about not wasting away your life living in the past? And how many have you heard about focusing too much on the future? Plenty? Living in the past or the future are both "I knew that" subjects. Parents, friends, and teachers have been warning us about that all our lives. So why do we require so many reminders? Why is it so easy to forget the simple principle—live for today?

While there are many reasons for this philosophical and theological amnesia, and plenty of blame to spread around, we must remember that Satan loves it when we get distracted from purposefully living each day for God. He wants us to dwell on the past—the "the good old days," and refuse to grow or change. He doesn't want us to "be transformed by the renewing of" our minds. He wants us to "rest on our laurels" and glory in the past! He loves it when we waste our time obsessing about missed opportunities, grieving about missed individuals, and dreaming about the way "it used to be."

I wonder if Jesus ever sat around doing that? Hey—His dreaming didn't just go back to Nazareth, Bethlehem, and Egypt, but to heaven, creation, and the "good old days" when it was just He, God, and the Holy Spirit! There's not even a hint of such thinking in the Gospels.

Satan also loves it when we postpone life. You know—when we think the only things worth living for are all in the future. So we put off happiness, fulfillment, and even a true walk with God until that "some day" arrives and it

I Knew That!

all "comes together" for us. Satan loves a procrastinator! When we "kill time" and see today as just something to "get through" as we move closer to some special future day or event, we squander one of the most precious blessings ever given to us. It's called "today." It's the only one we will ever have. There will never be another one exactly like this one. God gave it to us and He wants us to use it to grow and glorify Him, yet we let it slip through our fingers like a fistful of sand. Satan loves it! It puts us one step closer to belonging to him for eternity!

I wonder how much time Jesus spent thinking about the future? We know He did, but He certainly didn't dwell on it. How would it affect your life if you knew the exact date that you were going to die? What if you also knew that it was going to be a very violent and painful death? I suspect we'd all have a very difficult time not obsessing about the future. Yet Jesus didn't seem to spend much time thinking about it prior to His time in the garden the night before He was crucified. He was focused not fearful. I don't think of Him as ever being the wild-eyed fanatical extremist that some see. He seemed always to be calm, deliberate, and totally focused on the opportunity that each moment provided Him.

I would have been counting down the days to that date with the Romans. He didn't. I would have felt a sense of urgency that would have made me crazy with trying to cram everything I could into every day to the point of even resenting sleep. He didn't. I would have resented the future being cut short and forced myself to remember every event of the past. He didn't. I wouldn't be able to live for today because of fear for tomorrow. He didn't. For Him, every day was a special gift from God to be used to glorify God. It wasn't so much a matter of being productive each day as it was being godly each day. He showed us that it was possible to live one day at a time by seeing each day as the only part of God's plan that has been revealed to us. Use it or lose it!

Jesus seemed to know how to live life to the fullest. He didn't try to rush the future or dig up the past. He just lived each day for His Father and saw it as an opportunity to serve Him and anyone else He could. He didn't allow His life to be complicated by the pursuit and preservation of wealth, as we do. He wasn't concerned with His maintaining His comfort level, securing His castle, or climbing any ladders. He was God incarnate so every day was another chance to let people see and understand the Father.

We need to remember that the Jesus of the Bible is the Jesus of eternity. He didn't pretend to be something that He wasn't! The picture we get of Jesus in the Gospels it the picture of the real Son of God—the way He is—always. The writer of Hebrews said, "Jesus Christ is the same yesterday and today and forever" (13:8). So living and enjoying each individual day was not just something He started doing. That's the way He is! Before we even think about looking at what Solomon had to say about life, we need to look at what the Giver of life had to say about real living.

THOUGHTS FROM A WISER MAN ABOUT LIVING

Real living is uncomplicated living. Jesus calls us to simple living by pointing out simple truths that are classic "I knew that" truths. The Sermon on the Mount is the most profound sermon ever preached. In my opinion, what makes it so profound is its simplicity. It's proverbial, quotable, understandable, and simple! I hear people use expressions all the time that I'm sure they don't recognize as coming from the Sermon on the Mount.

People, often non-Christians, will say, "He's the salt of the earth," or "Let your light shine," or "the meek will inherit the earth," and have no idea that they are quoting Jesus. It's rich and timeless in its application, and one of the easiest passages in the whole Bible to understand. It is found in Matthew 5,6, and 7, and it has everything any of us might need to know concerning real living.

In chapter 5, Jesus calls all disciples to a heart-level and genuine relationship with God. God doesn't want legalistic self-righteousness like the Pharisees had. He wants a spiritual honesty that shows itself not only in right actions, but godly intent and holy consistency. Being spiritually inconsistent complicates life.

In chapter 6, He calls us all to genuine prayer. Prayer is first and foremost, an act of faith, but it is also what we do to build a relationship with God. Relationships are only as strong as the communication that is shared. Without prayer, we'd have no relationship with God. Jesus points out that we complicate and even threaten our relationship with God when we do spiritual things to be seen of men. So He not only challenges us to keep it simple and personal, He gave an example of how to do it. We call it the Lord's Prayer, but it's really an example of prayer.

Did you ever notice how simple that prayer was? Prayer needs to praise God, offer thanks, declare our obedience, ask for help, and ask for forgiveness as we forgive others (vv. 9-13). Keep it simple!

It should be no surprise to any of us that right after discussing prayer and doing religious things to be recognized by others, He goes strait to money. Our obsession with money clearly complicates our lives in a big way. As He points out, we allow money to become our master, and that is something God won't allow. There can be only one Master (vv. 19-24). Of course it's not really money as much as the things and stuff money can by. That is why He deals with it as something that complicates our lives. He declared,

> For this reason I say to you, do not be anxious for you life, as to what you will eat, or what you will drink; nor for you body, as to what you will put on. Is not life more than food, and the body than clothing?
> –v. 25

Anxiety robs us of the enjoyment of the day. We worry about so much that doesn't really count in the long run, and we fail to appreciate the day God gave us. We've worried it away. Jesus said that was a reflection on our lack of faith (v. 30). The way to live is to focus on God and His kingdom, and trust Him to give us what we need (v. 33).

He closes this call to simplicity and spirituality by saying, "So do not worry about tomorrow; for tomorrow will care for itself. Each day has enough trouble of its own" (v. 34). I've never heard anyone say it, but I believe this is from where the cliché "Live one day at a time" came. It's not just a *Power-of-Positive-Thinking* kind of thing or just a "Pollyanna" philosophy. It's the message of Jesus! If that is not a call to uncomplicated living I don't know what would be.

How do we do this? How do we live one day at a time and not allow ourselves to be overwhelmed with worries about the future? We must go back to prayer. Prayer is the key because prayer builds faith and trust in God. He is in charge and He will take care of His own—He promised. But prayer is also essential since it forces us to be thankful for what God has done for us. There is no contentment without thankfulness. There is no uncomplicated living without contentment. If we don't learn to be thankful we will never learn to live one day at a time.

THOUGHTS FROM A WISE MAN ABOUT LIVING

The wisest person ever to walk the earth was Jesus. His insights into living are the best and most dependable. There is, however, something to be said for listening to the advice of someone who learned all his lessons the hard way. Someone who could literally say, "Been there. Done that." Solomon was just such a person, and his experiential advice simply echoes Jesus.

The theme of Ecclesiastes seems to be "Enjoy each day and don't complicate things with selfishness." Solomon tried to find meaning in life by giving himself over to many different pursuits but none of them worked. He sought wisdom and knowledge, but ". . . in much wisdom there is much grief, and increasing knowledge results in increasing pain" (1:18). He sought pleasure and the pride of abundant possessions, but this "was vanity and striving after wind ...." (2:1-11). He tried to find fulfillment in his hard work, but that was just a waste of time, painful, and didn't even help him to sleep better (2:18-26).

He was quite possibly the wealthiest king in all history, certainly Jewish history, yet he said, "He who loves money will not be satisfied with money, nor he who loves abundance with its income. This too is vanity" (5:10). We each prove this to be true when we manage to live above our incomes no matter how many pay increases we receive. It's like he said in Proverbs 23:4-5:

> *Do not weary yourself to gain wealth,*
> *Cease from your consideration of it.*
> *When you set your eyes on it, it is gone.*
> *For wealth certainly makes itself wings*
> *Like an eagle that flies toward the heavens.*

Solomon mentions many pursuits that are meaningless for any person to focus on because they distract us from God and complicate our joy of living. At the same time, he does mention several things that we should do to get the most out of each day. They all seem to come down to one simple truth. He put it this way:

> *The conclusion, when all has been heard, is: fear God and keep His commandments, because this applies to every person. For God will bring every act to judgment, everything which is hidden, whether it is good or evil.*
> —Ecclesiastes 12:13-14

This is not only theologically simple, but simply practical. When we spend so much time and energy trying to "get around" what God wants us to do, we complicate our lives. When we trust in ourselves and not God, we complicate our lives. When we listen to the world's definition of happiness and ignore what Jesus and Solomon tell us, we complicate our lives. Even when we look "good" to everyone else, the hidden sin in our lives makes us miserable. Fearing God and keeping His commandments are really much easier.

I know what you're thinking—"I knew that!"

"I CAN'T DO IT!"

Remember the old joke "How do you eat an elephant?" The humorous but profound answer is "One bite at a time." Sometimes we are overwhelmed

I Knew That!

by the idea of living for Jesus every day of our lives for as long as we live. This barrier generally shrinks with age. When I was a teenager (sometime in the last millennium), I distinctly remember thinking that it was impossible for me to live a life that would please God. I saw the Christian walk as analogous to a tightrope walk: a very difficult balancing act that was doomed to fail sooner or later. I remember the frustration—the sense of failure, inadequacy, and despair. It was just too big of a job! I was just too imperfect!

Fortunately, receiving grace and understanding grace doesn't have to happen simultaneously! Like the old song says, "Grace is greater than all my sin," but it's also greater than my ability to comprehend its power. I'm forgiven even when I don't understand how and why it happens. Once that theological lightbulb finally turned on, I felt a lot better about my chances for success at this Christian living stuff! Still, I was overwhelmed by the size and length of the task before me. I was still trying to make it happen instead of letting it happen, and I still saw life as a long-term proposition. I was sure that living seventy-five to eighty years as a faithful Christian was simply unrealistic.

Yes, even way back then I knew that "with God all things are possible" and that "I can do all things through Him who strengthens me." It was not a matter of trusting in God but rather trusting in me! I didn't believe in me! Thankfully God did.

Here's the secret. Go look in the mirror and say to yourself, "My name is _____, and I am a sin-oholic." Say it two or three times and mean it. Then say, "My name is _____, and I am a sin-oholic—saved by the grace of God." After you've said that a few times add, "I can live for God today!" Say it until you mean it! Forget about tomorrow, next week, or next year. Forget about living for God for seventy or eighty years! Decide in your heart that you will *live for God today!* That's all that counts! On the average, you have just as much chance of dying long before seventy-five as after. You may already have been given all God intends for you to have! So don't worry about living for God in days you may never get! Live for Him today—it's all you have.

If that sounds suspiciously like something that would be said at an AA meeting or some drug rehabilitation group, it should. There is nothing more addicting and harder to overcome than sin. You've spent a lifetime enjoying it and its appeal won't ever go away completely. So—like any addiction, it must be dealt with one day at a time. One day is doable—a lifetime is incomprehensible. To even assume we have that time ahead of us is arrogance and probably fosters procrastination in us all. Don't go there—live for God today!

I knew that, didn't you? Why is it so hard to remember?

CHAPTER TEN
"Family Is Everything!"

    Second only to my relationship with God and Jesus, I am more thankful for my family relationship than anything else in life. I felt that nearly a quarter of a century ago when my firstborn cried out in the delivery room, but not with the passion, assurance, and conviction I have today. As I write this, we are just days away from when our firstborn has her firstborn and we become grandparents for the first time. That's part of the reason family means more to me than it ever has.

    We have such wonderful memories of life with our three children. God blessed us so much that it humbles me to the core. We've all had great health, we've had more material blessings than we can count, and we've all managed to grow up as a preacher's family and still praise God for the experience. Our children handled the "fish-bowl" living assuming everyone lived the same way. Of course, it helped that all three were (and are) serious extroverts. They didn't even realize that they were supposed to suffer from "The PK Syndrome," which is the psycho-talk that explains why ministers' kids tend to be so rotten. They gave their lives to Jesus as their own personal decision, and each one of them has been a whole lot more serious about their walk with Him than I was at their age. I can't wait to see what they will be like when they reach my age!

    Here is where I have to use tremendous restraint. You don't know how badly I want to go on and on about my family and how wonderful they are! So I'll fight the urge to brag and list all their accomplishments and qualities. I'll just sum it up with a quote I have used in sermons several times. Here it is, "You can find a better preacher, but you won't find a better preacher's wife or preacher's children than I have." There is some obvious prejudice in that statement, along with a lot of pride. But, I assure you it is a godly pride because God is the only One who deserves any credit.

I Knew That!

Family has always been important to me, but now I really know why. When my wife and I were young and raising three small children, their adulthood was so far away that it was incomprehensible. We couldn't imagine a time when they wouldn't be home, with us, and part of our everyday life. We couldn't imagine how it would feel to witness their being baptized into Jesus and see them grow spiritually. We had no ideal what it would be like to take them off and leave them at college, and then come home to a very empty and quiet house. And while we prayed that God would someday send them godly mates, we had no way of knowing how incredible that answered prayer would make us feel.

Back then, older folks would tell us, "family is everything," and by that they meant "keep your family at the top of your priorities list." I agreed! It sounded so right! I even preached it! Still, there were times when other things seemed more important—or at least more fun. Not bad things! Ministry is usually seen as a good thing—right? Being a police chaplain—saving lives, being in the center of crisis after crisis and really making a difference—that's good stuff, isn't it? Besides, there's plenty of time for family—later! Well, that's the way you think when you're young.

MAYBE IT IS AND MAYBE IT ISN'T!

Ignorance is bliss—sometimes. Until I learned differently, I thought I grew up in a wonderful family environment. I was loved and cared for. We had a lot of fun, with wonderful memories of trips, singing, Christmas, and Thanksgiving dinners. My mother worked hard and sacrificed a lot to provide for us, and she will always be one of the most loved and respected people in my life. But, I sure would have liked a dad.

That was back before they had descriptive labels like "single-parent home," or "latch-key kids," and "dysfunctional families." Actually, since my parents divorced when I was a baby, I never saw the really bad results of my father's alcoholism and abuse. I never knew him, even though the alcohol didn't kill him until I was 8 or 9. Still, my mother, sister, and brothers where great and I thought we had a wonderful family. I now know what I missed—what we all missed. That's not a complaint or whining! God took care of us and blessed us in many ways. That is one of the reasons my family means so much to me today. But today, however, my family has all the good things my birth family had and—the things it didn't have.

Family is important—even when it's not perfect or "normal," and who knows what is normal nowadays? Depending on the standard used, every family is probably "dysfunctional" to some degree. Actually, whether you

Family Is Everything!

have a family that's held together by nothing more than an address and some DNA, or a family that is close, supportive, and united in Christ, family really isn't everything!

But we've always been told that "Family is everything." I love the commitment that old axiom exudes, but it's just not true. Sure, family must be "A" top priority, but it must never be "THE" top priority. The kingdom of God must come first (Matthew 6:33). As the old song declares about Jesus, "He is my everything He is my all." Jesus must come first! He even warned us that He would likely break up families more than He would unite them. Remember His words in Matthew 10:34-38?

> *Do not think that I came to bring peace on earth; I did not come to bring peace, but a sword. For I came to* SET A MAN AGAINST HIS FATHER, AND A DAUGHTER AGAINST HER MOTHER, AND A DAUGHTER-IN-LAW AGAINST HER MOTHER-IN-LAW; *and* A MAN'S ENEMIES WILL BE THE MEMBERS OF HIS HOUSEHOLD. *He who loves father or mother more than Me is not worthy of Me. And he who does not take his cross and follow after Me is not worthy of Me.*

Accepting Jesus as the Messiah was a quick way to be disowned by your family in biblical times. It wasn't long before it even meant imprisonment and death. That is one of the reasons the early church had so many people who needed help with basic necessities of life. In Acts 2, they sold their land and possessions to help those in need (vv. 44-45). Many of these brothers had been "kicked out" of their families and lost their jobs. They were heretics and blasphemers to their Jewish relatives.

As important as family is, your soul is still the most valuable possession you have. There is absolutely nothing more important than making sure that your soul is heaven bound. Jesus said it was more important than gaining the "whole world" (Matthew 16:26). Your soul is eternal and not only that, it cost a great deal for Jesus to redeem it. It must take top priority.

It must also be remembered that sometimes family is something to overcome, rather than something that supports you. Even today, there are many that are like the early Christians who became disciples and lost their families. If someone comes from an abusive family or a seriously ungodly family, he becomes a Christian in spite of his family and not because of them. Occasionally someone comes to Jesus from a religion that is very anti-Christ, and they must be more loyal to Him than to their own family. Many times the church becomes their new family. Even then, as wonderful as the church is, it's not "everything" or more important than our personal walk with God.

While it's not everything—it's still important. Like I mentioned at the beginning, for me, family is second only to my relationship with God. That makes it pretty important, right? It can and should be one of the most wonderful blessings in our entire lives. We receive love and support. We have a sense of belonging, a sense of heritage, and a sense of connectedness. Our most precious memories usually involve family. Our strongest sense of responsibility is usually centered on our family. Jesus' family was important to Him, even as He hung dying on the cross. His dying wish was for John to take care of His mother (John 19:26-27).

The Bible is full of accounts about families. From Adam and Eve to Priscilla and Aquila, the Word of God is a record of good and bad families, families that followed God's will and families that rebelled against His will. It's safe to say that no one mentioned in the Bible was without a family—except for Adam—for a short period of time.

One of the largest families mentioned in the Bible was the family of Solomon. His household alone was the size of some small nations. So when he wrote Proverbs, he had a great deal to say about the importance of family. One of my personal favorites is Proverbs 27:8: "Like a bird that wanders from her nest, So is a man who wanders from his home." What a picturesque metaphor! I can clearly imagine the little baby bird getting separated from the security of the nest and parental oversight. It's helpless, defenseless, and alone. So is the person who leaves home unprepared, dependent, and not ready for flight. Kind of like the first week of college for many freshmen.

I have two shelves of my personal library devoted to nothing but marriage and family books. How many books have been written through the years on that subject? Countless! I could have a bibliography a mile long on this subject, but let's limit it to just one—Proverbs. Proverbs is like a man-made swimming pool. You can swim in the deep or you can swim in the shallow. Both get you wet, but one is easier than the other. I like easy. Solomon's proverbs seem to say two simple (not necessarily shallow) things. All families have problems, but all families also have blessings.

FAMILY PROBLEMS OF THE SON-TYPE

It's been passed around so many times that I can't begin to figure out who said it first, but my favorite "Redneck" joke is, "You know you're a redneck if your family tree doesn't fork!" The irony is that while that is humorous, it is also true of many monarchies in Europe. I guess royalty and "ruralty" are not so far apart after all.

Family Is Everything!

Another play on words with the family tree analogy is the saying, "Every family tree has some sap in it." No family is perfect or problem free. Even Jesus had some difficulty being accepted by His own siblings. Families are made up of humans who share a common gene pool, and that doesn't guarantee one minute of peace, cooperation, and compatibility. One of the first two brothers who ever lived murdered the other one. From Jacob's twelve boys to the Prodigal son, the Bible is replete with parent-child problems; and divorce has been rampant since the time of Moses. There's nothing new about family problems. It's just that there are more books, tapes, and seminars available to help today and 24/7 news to report on all the failures.

Solomon said, "He who troubles his own house will inherit wind. . . ." (Proverbs 11:29). As mentioned before, he may be one of the world's best experts on family problems. He had an army of wives and children all standing in line to receive their "cut" of his famous wealth, and he makes it clear that the troublemaker will get only a big goose egg. If one of history's wisest men had family trouble, why would we possibly believe that we are exempt?

Solomon seems to have written Proverbs from the viewpoint of a man. Most of the family troubles he mentions are either directed to sons or to women. I guess his daughters were all obedient and well behaved. Even if they weren't, sons tend to overshadow daughters in their need for guidance and direction. They just seem to be a little slower on the learning curve. I like the story of the five-year-old boy challenging his five-year-old buddy with, "My Dad can beat up your Dad!" To which his opponent replied, "Big deal! So can my mother!" NOT the kind of thing a Dad wants to hear.

There are several passages in Proverbs that speak directly to sons.

> *A wise son makes a father glad,*
> *But a foolish man despises his mother.*
> –Proverbs 15:20

That sounds like the classic paternal inconsistency. Like when a Dad says, "That's *my* boy," after the boy makes a touchdown, but then turns around and says to his wife, "What has *your* boy done?" when the notice to meet the school principal arrives. Of course, to all dads, a wise son is one who is wise enough to do what you would do if you were in his place.

> *He who sires a fool does so to his sorrow,*
> *And the father of a fool has no joy.*
> –Proverbs 17:21

I Knew That!

> *A foolish son is a grief to his father,*
> *And bitterness to her who bore him.*
> —Proverbs 17:25

> *He who curses his father or his mother,*
> *His lamp will go out in time of darkness.*
> —Proverbs 20:20

There is no pain for parents like the pain of disappointment in a son or a daughter. In these proverbs, Solomon is probably talking about adult children, not the silly, hard knocks of growing up that each child must go through. He's referring to that pain that comes from seeing poor choices made by children you know you raised to know better. Moms and dads may become "empty nesters," as we call it now, but they never stop being moms and dads. They never lose that love and concern for their children, and they never get so removed by miles or times as not to care when some poor decision is made. That is why Solomon uses words like "grief" and "bitterness" to describe the heartache of parents with troublesome children.

One of the worst "I knew that's" that any of us will ever have is the realization that we should have invested ourselves more in the rearing of our children. We only get one chance at it, and we must devote ourselves to raising them with all the love, training, and attention we can give. It's not like we don't know it's important, but like all "I knew that" things, it just seems to take us by surprise to realize that our children are grown and out of our influence, and all the things we "intended" to do, are empty hopes. Establish priorities, especially as God directs, and then commit to them. Do all you can while you can, because the days will slip by before you know it. (Of course, you knew that!)

One other observation I want to make is simply that even the best of children, from the best of families, grow up and make poor choices. Proverbs 22:6 was intended to be an encouragement not a guilt trip. "Train up a child in the way he should go, Even when he is old he will not depart from it." Solomon was not, I believe, declaring an absolute guarantee. He was simply stating the obvious. Do your best, do it right, and it will pay off! But remember, Satan will never stop working on your kids anymore than he stops working on you. And there is no amount of spiritual training that removes temptation, the pull of sin, or the freedom of choice. Minds can and are changed at any age. This passage has been abused too many times and in many cases has lulled parents into a false sense of security about their own adult children.

I wonder if Jesse felt like a failure every time David, the "man after God's own heart," slipped up and needed to repent?

FAMILY PROBLEMS OF THE FEMALE-TYPE

I wonder what all those wives and concubines thought about Solomon. Wouldn't you love to have been the proverbial "fly on the wall" in their rooms when the talking started? Of course, when there are a thousand women with whom to compare notes, there were probably some who only saw him once or twice a year (or maybe once every three years for dinner). We'll never know what their "insights to men" might have been. But Solomon recorded some of his thoughts about women problems.

> *As a ring of gold in a swine's snout*
> *So is a beautiful woman who lacks discretion.*
> —Proverbs 11:22

Oh the things that would be fun to say at this point! The illustrations I would love to use! The puns! The blond jokes! Let me just say . . . here's the second passage.

> *It is better to live in a corner of a roof*
> *Than in a house shared with a contentious woman.*
> —Proverbs 21:9

I knew there was some reason he built a separate house for all the ladies in his family rather than let them live in the same house with him. Actually, this sounds like a line from *Fiddler on the Roof*. Why fight an unwinnable battle? Go camp on the roof, it will be a lot more peaceful. Or even better, go live in the desert.

> *It is better to live in a desert land*
> *Than with a contentious and vexing woman.*
> —Proverbs 21:19

Now remember, he's talking about a "contentious" or quarrelsome woman, so that means he's not talking about your situation. Right? The following is my favorite passage about this unusual and probably non-existent family problem.

> *A constant dripping on a day of steady rain*
> *And a contentious woman are alike;*
> *He who would restrain her restrains the wind,*
> *And grasps oil with his right hand.*
>   –Proverbs 27:15-16

I'm sure there would be many proverbs about men and husbands if the book had been written by a woman. But, Proverbs was written by a man—and not just any man—the king of Israel. While there is no attempt at gender balance, the reality of marital strife comes through loud and clear. Every marriage struggles occasionally. That is merely a fact of life. The beauty is that it's in working through these struggles—these times of stress that every relationship grows and is strengthened. It's problem solving—together! It's learning, compromising, understanding, and accepting—together! It's the stuff of which marital cement is made.

Not all nagging is negative. Sometimes it's needed. Remember the story Jesus told to stress the importance of persistence in prayer? He told of a judge who wasn't particularly God-fearing, but who was pestered by a widow to help her. He finally relented and said, ". . . because this widow bothers me, I will give her legal protection, otherwise by continually coming she will wear me out" (Luke 18:1-8). She was "a constant dripping" to that judge and she finally changed his mind. Jesus was clearly teaching the need for persistence in our petitions to God. But of course, persistence is one thing while being contentious is another.

Many a mate became a child of God because of a persistent wife or husband. Few, however, have decided to live for Jesus because of a contentious spouse.

FAMILY BLESSINGS

Sometimes I talk with so many clichés that I feel like a reincarnated Will Rogers. When someone asked me how I'm doing, I usually say, "If I was any better it would be a sin!" It's a silly little greeting, but like a lot of things, there's more truth to it than what hits the ear. I often feel a little guilty because God has blessed me so much. I've already either ignored or taken for granted so many of His good gifts, that if He blessed me any more, I'd really be guilty of ungratefulness.

One of the really wonderful blessings that comes with being a new "empty nester" is having the time to reflect on how truly blessed I am. I am more thankful for my family than I have ever been in my life. It's a wonderful mixture of being proud and humble at the same time. Each one of my adult children is everything I ever hoped and prayed he or she would be. Most of all, they love God, have a faithful walk with His Son, and have found mates who are the same. The only thing that tops all that is the loving wife with whom God has aloud me to spend the last thirty years of my life.

Solomon speaks to this in many of his proverbs. In reflecting on children he said,

> *A wise son makes a father glad. . . .*
> —Proverbs 10:1

> *Hear, my son, your father's instruction*
> *And do not forsake your mother's teaching;*
> *Indeed, they are a graceful wreath to your head*
> *And ornaments about your neck*
> —Proverbs 1:8-9

> *Grandchildren are the crown of old men*
> *And the glory of sons is their fathers.*
> —Proverbs 17:6

> *The father of the righteous will greatly rejoice,*
> *And he who sires a wise son will be glad in him.*
> *Let your father and your mother be glad,*
> *And let her rejoice who gave birth to you.*
> *Give me your heart, my son,*
> *And let your eyes delight in my ways*
> —Proverbs 23:24-26

> *An excellent wife is the crown of her husband. . . .*
> —Proverbs 12:4

> *He who finds a wife finds a good thing*
> *And obtains favor from the LORD.*
> —Proverbs 18:22

I Knew That!

> *An excellent wife, who can find?*
> *For her worth is far above jewels....*
> *Her children rise up and bless her;*
> *Her husband also, and he praises her....*
> *Charm is deceitful and beauty is vain,*
> *But a woman who fears the LORD, she shall be praised.*
> *—Proverbs 31:10-30*

I am sitting in my office in the church building. I am surrounded by ministry memorabilia from almost thirty years. Books, pictures, mugs, awards, plaques, diplomas, trinkets, gifts, files, folders, collections, souvenirs, trophies, and yes, junk. Just looking around the room is a trip down memory lane any time I want it. It's my history! To a certain degree, it's my accomplishments! After all, there's one shelf devoted to just the books that I have written! There are more stories in the books, pictures, and knick-knacks loading each shelf than I could tell in any one book! Every item, from the Elvis stamp to the can of possum meat, fills me with warm memories and feeling for the people and events behind each one. (The roll of John Wayne Toilet Tissue may be an exception.)

There is nothing in this room that fills me with more gladness or that is more of an ornament around my neck than my three Christian children and my godly wife of over thirty years. And, since the writing of this book spans several months, there is now a little fellow who is "the crown of" this old man—my first grandson, Joshua.

I don't share that to brag—though it's hard not to. I share it to remind you that family really is everything. And while you shake your head and say, "I knew that," if you don't devote yourself to raising those children as best you can, you may not have the same kind of feelings as I've just described to you when you are an "empty nester" or when you become a grandparent for the first time.

If I had read all this thirty years ago, I would have said, "I knew that," too. If you want to look across the dinner table at your spouse of three decades and feel a sense of love and thankfulness that is greater than you ever dreamed, it will take a lot more "I did that" than "I knew that" in your life. No one ever said it would be easy. In fact, there is little about any relationship that is easy. It takes effort, care, and consistency. Your marriage and your parenting will never rise above your level of thoughtfulness. They will only be as strong as your ability to remember how important they are and your willingness to do the little things—the daily things—that keep them eternally precious to you.

Family Is Everything!

The key to making this happen is beautifully described in the following poem.

*How God must love a friendly home
Which has a warming smile,
To welcome everyone who comes
To bide a little while!*

*How God must love a happy home
Where song and laughter show,
Hearts full of joyous certainty
That life means ways to grow!*

*How God must love a loyal home
Serenely sound and sure!
When troubles come to those within,
They still can feel secure.*

*How God must love a Christian home
Where faith and love attest
That every moment, every hour,
He is the honored Guest!*[1]

"JUST A LITTLE TALK WITH JESUS"
"Lord, from the very beginning of my marriage I wanted to be the best mate I possibly could. The love was always there—it's just that I occasionally allowed myself to get distracted by career, hobbies, accumulating things—even church work. And through the years—as I grew, I remembered my commitment, and I renewed my efforts to be a more thoughtful and loving mate—but I still allowed selfishness to rule every now and then. But I always tried to keep my marriage as a high priority."

And He said, "I knew that!"

"And Lord, those precious children you gave us—so healthy, so sweet, and so lovable, were always the focus of my life. It's just that when they were little—I was still so young, so full of life, so in search of adventure, and so wanting to impress everyone else with my new toys. I wanted promotions. I wanted raises in pay. I wanted all the good things of life for my family. Those

I Knew That!

precious little souls only belonged to me for a short while, and occasionally I forgot how important they were and how quickly the time would pass. We sang about Jesus and talked about His Word. We prayed to the Father every day. I could have done more—I wanted to do more, but—sometimes—every now and then—well, they were always important—I just needed a few reminders. Sometimes I feel like they turned out so well in spite of me more than because of me. I tried my best, but . . ."

And He said, "I knew that."

"I have always been a sinner. I know that I have disappointed You many times. I also know that You have been very patient with me. You gave me opportunities to grow, to reflect, to learn, and to try harder. You allowed me to learn more about love by giving me a godly wife and wonderful children, who loved me, supported me, and helped me grow up. As I watched them become mature Christians, choose Christian mates, and start their own families, I am humbled by Your blessings. I am humbled by the favor You have shown us. I am humbled by Your grace, Your providential guidance, and Your love. I don't deserve it—I never have and never will! I am a sinner! I forget what my priorities should be. I forget the price You paid to save me. I forget how blessed I am and how thankful I must be! There have been too many 'I knew that's' in my life! Lord, I need Your forgiveness constantly. I love You, I trust You, and I give You the glory for every thing."

*And He said, "I knew that," but for Him—
it's a statement of fact, not a reminder.*

NOTE
1. Doan, *Speaker's Sourcebook*, p. 419.

Bibliography

Barclay, William. *The Letters to the Corinthians.* The Daily Study Bible Series. Philadelphia: Westminster, 1975.

Doan, Eleanor. *Speaker's Sourcebook.* Grand Rapids: Zondervan, 1960.

"1 Corinthians." *The Expositor's Bible Commentary.* Vol. 10. Grand Rapids: Zondervan, 1991.

"Proverbs." *The Expositor's Bible Commentary.* Vol. 5. Grand Rapids: Zondervan, 1991.

Harrison, Everett F. *A Short Life of Christ.* Grand Rapids: Eerdmans, 1968.

Keil, C.F., and F. Delitzch. *Commentary on the Old Testament.* Vol. VI. Grand Rapids: Eerdmans, 1980.

McGinnis, Alan Loy. *The Friendship Factor.* Minneapolis: Augsburg, 1979.

Tan, Paul Lee, *Encyclopedia of 7700 Illustrations: Signs of the Times.* Rockville, MD: Assurance Publishers, 1979.

Vine, W.E., *Expository Dictionary of New Testament Words.* Old Tappan, NJ: Revell, 1966 edition.

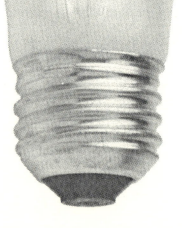
The father of the righteous will greatly rejoice

About the Author

Born in the Nation's Capital, Mike Root left home at thirteen to attend school in Georgia at Georgia Christian School, were he graduated in 1970. He received a BA in Bible from Harding University and spent a year working there as an Admissions Counselor. His career as a pulpit minister includes: a two-year ministry in Benton, Arkansas, were he was also the Youth Minister; a thirteen-year ministry with the Fairfax Church of Christ in Fairfax, Virginia, just outside of Washington, D.C., where he also served as a police chaplain with the Fairfax County Police Department; and an eight-year ministry with the Altamesa Church of Christ in Fort Worth, Texas. Since March of 1998, he has been the pulpit minister with the Antioch Church of Christ in Nashville, Tennessee.

Mike has a Master of Arts degree in History from George Mason University and a Master of Theology degree from Trinity Theological Seminary. He has a novel entitled *Rev*, which is based on his experiences as a police chaplain. He has four other books that have been published by College Press Publishing entitled *Spilt Grape Juice, Life's Cobwebs, Unbroken Bread, and Empty Baskets*. He has published articles in *The Christian Chronicle, Gospel Advocate, Church & Family, Image Magazine, and Wineskins*. He has taught seminars, workshops, and had speaking appointments in twenty-eight states and three foreign countries. He has also been on the lectureship programs of several Christian universities.

He is a Self-Defense Instructor and an avid bowhunter. His wife of thirty years is the former Donna Sue Curtis; and they have three children: Jonathan, who is in theater, Elizabeth is an RN and married to Chad Milom, and Deborah is married to Pat Bills, who is a Youth Minister with the Saturn Road church in Dallas, Texas. They are the parents of Mike's first grandson, Joshua Hunter Bills.

Printed in the United States
1082700006B/310-510